MEDITERRANEO EDITIONS

Cretan Cookery
Mum's 200 recipes

Text & styling by
STELLA KALOGERAKI

Layout
VANGELIS PAPIOMYTOGLOU

DTP
NATASSA ANTONAKI

Translation
JILL PITTINGER

Copyright 2005
MEDITERRANEO EDITIONS
Tel. +3028310 21590, Fax: +3028310 21591

www.mediterraneo.gr

ISBN: 960-8227-54-2

Cretan Cookery

Mum's 200 recipes

MEAT AND MINCED MEAT

SEAFOOD & FISH

SALADS

Country salad

Wash the vegetables well and cut them into small pieces. Mix on a plate and add the feta, olives and oil. Season with salt and the salad is ready. A little oregano can also be scattered over the feta, for a stronger flavour.

1 tomato
1 cucumber
1 slice feta cheese
½ onion
Black olives
2-3 tbs olive oil
Salt

Skordalia

Pound the garlic in a mortar until it is well crushed. Add the salt and the bread, having first sprinkled the latter with a little water. Slowly, and alternately, add the oil, lemon and vinegar. Beat well until the skordalia acquires the preferred, soft consistency.

6 cloves of garlic
1 cup bread crusts
Salt
Juice of 1 lemon
2 tsp vinegar
1 cup olive oil

Dakos or Koukouvayia

Soak the rusk in water and then wrap it in a clean tea towel to dry. Mince the tomato and the feta and place on top of the rusk. Add the oil, salt, oregano and if liked, a little finely chopped onion.

1 barley rusk

1 tomato

1 slice feta cheese

2-3 tbs olive oil

Salt

1 onion

Oregano

Aubergine salad

Prick the aubergines with a fork and roast over charcoal or under a grill. When they are ready, remove the skins and puree the flesh in a blender. Add the lemon, salt, garlic and - slowly – the oil. Finally, if liked, add a few chopped walnuts.

1 kg round aubergines

1 cup olive oil

Juice of 1 lemon

2 crushed cloves of garlic

Salt

5-6 chopped walnuts (optional)

Taramosalata

Crumble the bread and place in a bowl with the taramas. Begin beating (use a mixer), and adding olive oil and lemon juice alternately in small quantities, until the mixture is soft and creamy. If liked, add a small amount of chopped walnuts and serve garnished with black olives.

150 gr taramas (fish roe)

300 gr stale bread

2 tbs lemon juice

1 cup olive oil

2-3 walnuts

Pickled artichokes

Clean the artichokes, cut into pieces if large, and place in a bowl with water and the lemon juice, to prevent them from discolouring. Prepare the pickling solution as follows: Add a whole egg to some water, and then begin to add salt until the egg rises to the surface and acquires a diameter the size of a 2 Euro piece. The solution is now ready. Add the cleaned artichokes and leave them covered for one day. On the following day drain off the solution, place the artichokes in a glass container and cover them with oil. Close the container well and store in a cool place. Serve with a little lemon juice or vinegar.

Little whole artichokes, or large ones cut into four

Olive oil

Vinegar

Salt

Lemon juice

Zatziki

1 kg strained
yogurt
1 large cucumber
5 cloves of garlic
1 bunch of dill
½ cup olive oil
Salt, pepper

Clean, grate
and drain the
cucumber. Pound
the garlic in a
mortar with the
salt. In a bowl,
mix together the
yogurt, garlic,
finely chopped
dill, pepper and oil.
Beat well in a mixer
or by hand and
the zatziki is ready.
Cover and store in
the refrigerator.

SAUCES

Oil and lemon dressing

Mix together the ingredients and beat well; the sauce is ready. If a more piquant taste is desired, add 1 tsp mustard. Excellent with grilled or baked fish, vegetables or salads.

1 cup olive oil

4 tbs lemon juice

½ tsp salt

1 tsp mustard (optional)

Egg and lemon (avgolemono)

Beat the eggs and very slowly add the lemon juice. Continue to beat while gradually adding some of the liquid. Finally, add the sauce to the pan containing the food and shake it so that the sauce is distributed around it.

2 eggs

Juice of two lemons

1-2 cups of liquid from the dish you are making

Oil and vinegar dressing

Mix together the ingredients and beat well. The sauce is ready. Use with salads or boiled vegetables.

1 cup olive oil
1/2 cup vinegar
Salt

Béchamel

Gently warm the milk. Place the butter in a pan and when it has just melted, add the flour. Mix well together and continue to beat while beginning to add the milk. Add the salt, pepper and nutmeg and stir over the heat until the sauce thickens and is smooth in consistency. When it has cooled slightly, add the eggs and beat well again.

3 cups milk
3 tbs butter
7 tbs flour or cornflour
Salt, pepper, nutmeg
2 eggs

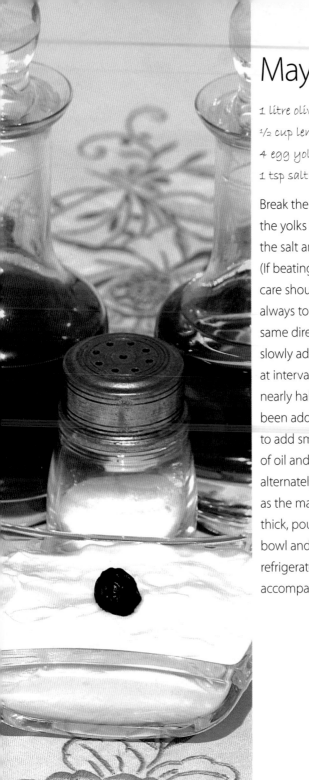

Mayonnaise

1 litre olive oil
½ cup lemon juice
4 egg yolks
1 tsp salt

Break the eggs, place the yolks in a bowl with the salt and beat well. (If beating by hand, care should be taken always to beat in the same direction). Now slowly add oil, beating at intervals. When nearly half the oil has been added, begin to add small amounts of oil and lemon juice alternately. As soon as the mayonnaise is thick, pour it into a glass bowl and store in the refrigerator. An excellent accompaniment to fish.

PIES

Spinach pie

Clean the spinach and the leeks, and cut them up. Finely chop the dill and the onions. Heat the oil in a pan and sautι together the onions, leeks, dill and spinach. Add the salt and pepper, reduce the heat and leave for a few minutes to soften, without adding water. Remove the pan from the heat and when the mixture is cold, add the crumbled feta and the beaten eggs.

Make the pastry as follows: place the flour in a bowl, make a well in the centre, and add the salt, oil, vinegar and (gradually) water to make a smooth dough. Form into a ball, cover and leave to rest for ½-1 hour. Then divide into four pieces and roll out into evenly-sized, thin sheets. Place one of these in a baking dish, the base and sides of which have been oiled. Brush the surface of the sheet with oil and add another piece of pastry. Now add the filling on top of the pastry, and cover with the two remaining sheets, oiling the surface of each. Press together the edges of the upper and lower sheets to seal. Brush with oil, sprinkle over the sesame and bake in a preheated oven for about 1 hour.

Pastry:
½ kg flour
½ cup olive oil
1 cup water
1 tsp salt
2 tbs vinegar
Sesame

Filling:
1 kg spinach
2 leeks
4 fresh spring onions
1 bunch dill
3 eggs
250 gr feta
Salt, pepper
1 cup olive oil

Cheese pie

Mix together the ingredients for the pastry and form the dough into a ball; cover and leave for a little while 'to rest'. Prepare the filling by mixing all the ingredients (except for one egg) together in a bowl. Now divide the pastry into two pieces and roll them out into two sheets. Lay one sheet in an oiled baking dish so that it extends up the sides, place the filling on top and then lay the other sheet of pastry over it. Press the two sheets well together to close the pie, brush the top with the remaining beaten egg and place the dish in a preheated oven. Leave to bake for about 1 hour.

Fyllo pastry:
1/2 kg flour
1 carton of yogurt
1 cup butter or oil

Filling:
1/2 kg feta cheese
3 eggs
1 cup milk
3 tbs flour or semolina
2 tbs olive oil

Leek pie

Prepare the pastry (as for spinach pie) and let it rest. Wash and chop the leeks. Mix well together in a bowl with the crumbled feta, beaten eggs, milk, oil, salt and pepper. Make four sheets of pastry and place two in a baking dish, then add the filling and place two sheets on top as in the previous recipe. Brush the top of the pie with 1 beaten egg and bake in a preheated oven for about 1 hour.

Pastry:
1/2 kg flour
1/2 cup olive oil
1 cup water
1 tsp salt
2 tbs vinegar
Sesame

Filling:
1 kg leeks
6 eggs
300 gr feta
2 cups milk
Salt, pepper
1/2 cup olive oil

Chicken pie

1 chicken
½ kg onions
3 eggs
½ cup milk
1 cup grated cheese
Salt, pepper, nutmeg
½ cup olive oil
10 sheets fyllo pastry

Wash the chicken and place in a saucepan with water to boil. Add the onions, cut into rounds, and salt. When the chicken is tender, remove it and leave the onions to continue boiling until they are soft and the liquid reduced. Cut up the chicken, removing skin and bones and then tear it into strips using your hands. When the liquid containing the onions has reduced, add the milk and the chicken. Stir well together and bring to the boil once or twice. Remove from the heat, add the eggs, cheese, salt pepper and nutmeg and mix well. Oil the baking dish and line with 7 sheets of fyllo, each of which has been oiled separately. Pour in the mixture, cover with the remaining sheets of fyllo (also oiled separately) and finally brush the surface of the pie with oil. Cut through the pastry into portions and bake in a moderate oven for about 1 hour.

Minced beef pie

Make the pastry as follows: place the flour in a bowl, make a well in the centre, and add the salt, oil, vinegar and (gradually) water to make a smooth dough. Form into a ball, cover and leave to rest for ½-1 hour. Meanwhile, make the filling: heat the oil in a pan and sautı the finely chopped onions. Add the minced beef and stir constantly. Add a cup of water, the salt, pepper and nutmeg and allow to boil. When the meat is done, remove from the heat and after it has cooled add the cheese, the egg yolks, and the well-beaten whites. Stir well together. Cut the pastry into four pieces and roll them out into four thin sheets, two of which should be slightly larger. Oil the base and sides of a baking dish and line it with

Pastry:

½ kg flour

½ cup olive oil

1 cup water

1 tsp salt

2 tbs vinegar

Sesame

Filling:

1 kg minced beef

4 onions

1 cup grated parmesan cheese

4 eggs

salt, pepper, nutmeg

½ cup olive oil

Rice pie

Parboil the rice, drain and rinse it with cold water. Place in a bowl and add the salt, the beaten eggs, the grated cheese and 3 tbs of the oil. Mix well together. Place three sheets of fyllo in an oiled dish, add a little of the filling on top and then alternately 3 more sheets of fyllo and a layer of filling. Each time a sheet of pastry is added its surface should be oiled. Score the surface of the pie and bake in a preheated oven for about 1 hour.

½ kg rice
9 eggs
½ kg cheese
Salt
1 cup olive oil
10 sheets of fyllo

the two larger sheets, oiling the surface of each. Add the filling and cover with the two remaining sheets, which have also been oiled. Press together the edges of the upper and lower sheets to seal, score the surface into portions, brush with oil and bake in a preheated oven for about 1 hour.

Easter meat pie

Cut up the meat, wash and drain it, and then season with salt and pepper. Leave to marinate for one hour sprinkled with the lemon juice. Now simmer it in a saucepan over a low heat for about ½ hour. Remove from the heat and strain. Mix the cheeses in a separate bowl. Finely chop the mint.

Make the pastry as follows: Sieve the flour together with the salt into a bowl and make a little well in the centre. Dissolve the yeast in a little warm water and add to the flour together with the egg and the milk. Mix into a firm dough, cover, and leave in a warm place. When the dough has risen, divide it into two and roll out into two sheets. Place one into an oiled baking dish so that it covers the sides and hangs over the edges. Now add the filling as follows: a layer of meat, a layer of cheese, then the mint (if desired, the fillings can be divided into two and this procedure carried out twice). Pour over the staka (thick cream) and cover with the second sheet of pastry. Wet your fingers and join the edges of the upper and lower sheet, pressing together the overhang and the top sheet to form a good seal. Brush the pie with beaten egg, sprinkle with sesame and bake in a preheated oven at 190 C for about ½ hour, until the pie has browned.

Filling:

1 ½ kg lamb

½ kg myzithra or anthotyro cheese

300 gr soft curd cheese

3 tbs finely chopped mint

4 tbs staka (thick cream)

Juice of 1 lemon

Salt, pepper

Pastry:

½ kg flour

1 envelope yeast

1 cup milk

1 egg

Pinch of salt

Courgette pie

Filling:
1 ½ kg green courgettes
½ kg feta
½ kg cream cheese
5 eggs, lightly beaten
A few mint leaves
Salt

Pastry:
½ kg flour
1 cup margarine
1 cup yogurt

Grate the courgettes, sprinkle them with salt and leave them in a sieve to drain. Press out the water from them with your hands. Meanwhile, crumble the cheese and mix together with the beaten eggs. Mix together the courgettes with the cheese, finely chop and add the mint. Make the pastry as follows: beat together the margarine and yogurt in a bowl and add the flour. Knead into a dough suitable for rolling out into sheets. Form the dough into a ball, cover with a tea towel and leave to rest for ½ hour.

Divide the dough into two parts, one a little larger. Roll out into two sheets and spread the larger of the two in a buttered or oiled baking dish, so that the pastry covers the sides of the dish and hangs over. Spread the filling on top of the pastry and cover with the second sheet, pressing together the top and bottom sheets to seal. Oil the surface, score it and sprinkle over the sesame. Bake the pie in a moderate oven until the surface is well-browned.

Little pies filled with wild greens, fried

Wash the greens, dill and onions well and chop them. Place the oil in a pan and as soon as it has heated sautı the onions. Add the dill, greens, salt, pepper and two cups of water. Cover the pan and let the mixture cook for about ½ hour. When it is ready, transfer to a sieve and leave to drain well. Meanwhile make the pastry as follows: place the flour with the salt in a bowl and make a well in the centre. Add the oil and lemon juice and mix together, adding water slowly to form an even, moderately soft dough. Shape into a ball, cover with a cloth and leave to rest for ½ hour. Thereafter, roll out into a very thin sheet and use a glass with a diameter of about 8 cms to cut out rounds. Place 1 tbs of the greens on each round and fold over the pastry to form a half-moon shape. Press together the edges with a fork to seal them and fry the pastries in a generous amount of boiling oil, taking care to brown them on both sides. Remove from the pan and place on kitchen paper on a plate, in order to drain off the oil.

Filling:

1 kg wild greens (or spinach)

1 bunch dill

4 fresh spring onions

½ cup oil

Salt, pepper

Pastry:

½ kg flour

1 cup water

3 tbs oil

2 tbs lemon juice

Salt

Oil for frying

EGGS

Omelette with wild greens

Pick over the greens, wash them well and boil them in water to which a little salt has been added. When they are ready strain them, cut them into small pieces and mix together with the crumbled cheese. Heat the oil to a high temperature in the frying pan and add half of the eggs. When the mixture sets, spread the greens on top of it and then add the remaining eggs. Turn the omelette to cook well on both sides.

½ kg asparagus or sweet wild greens

5 eggs

250 gr crumbled feta cheese

Salt, pepper

Olive oil for frying

Fried eggs with tomato sauce

5 eggs

4-5 ripe tomatoes

250 gr feta or kefalotyri cheese

Salt, pepper

Olive oil for frying

Wash the tomatoes and pass them through a sieve. Place the oil in a frying pan and bring to a high temperature. Add the tomatoes, salt and pepper; allow to cook and form a sauce. Then add the cheese, grated, and the eggs, taking care not to break them. When the whites have set, the dish is ready. Remove from the heat and serve each egg with a little sauce.

Omelette with courgettes

Wash the courgettes, cut them into medium rounds and fry them. Place on kitchen paper to drain. Finely chop the onions, sautı them in a little oil and add the courgettes. Beat the eggs and add the milk and flour, stirring it into the mixture. Add the eggs to the pan, stir briefly, season well and cook the omelette well on both sides.

1 kg small courgettes
6 eggs
1 onion
Salt, pepper
2 tbs milk
2 tbs flour
Olive oil for frying

Omelette with eggs and tomatoes (strapatsada)

1 kg tomatoes
5 eggs
Salt, pepper
1/2 cup feta cheese
1/2 cup oil

Wash the tomatoes and pass them through a sieve. Beat the eggs, mix together with the tomatoes and season well. Heat the oil to a high temperature in a pan and add the mixture. Stir well, and add the grated cheese when it has cooked.

Omelette with artichokes

Wash and clean the artichokes and place them in a bowl of water to which lemon juice has been added so that they do not discolour. Then cut them into small pieces and cook them in a pan without oil, until they have softened a little. Now add the oil and sautı them well. Beat the eggs and add them to the pan. Season well and turn the omelette to cook it on both sides.

4 eggs
3 artichokes
1 lemon
Salt, pepper
Olive oil for frying

Omelette with asparagus and avronies

Prepare the asparagus and avronies, retaining only the tender parts. Wash them well and boil until they are soft. Place the oil in a pan and when it is very hot add the boiled vegetables, beaten eggs, salt and pepper. Turn the omelette to cook it well on both sides.

½ kg asparagus

1 bunch avronies

6 eggs

4-5 tbs olive oil

Salt, pepper

PULSES

Bean soup

Soak the beans in water overnight to soften them. Next morning, change the water and boil them for about 15 minutes. Change the water again and add the onions, celery and finely chopped green peppers, chopped tomatoes, salt, pepper and oil. Allow all to boil for 20 minutes and then add the carrots cut into rounds. Remove from the heat after about ½ hour, when the beans have cooked and the sauce has thickened.

½ kg beans
½ kg tomatoes
2 green peppers
2 carrots
2 onions
Celery
Salt, pepper
1 cup olive oil

Giant dried beans in the oven

Soak the beans in water overnight to soften them. The following morning, rinse them and put them to boil in a pan of water for half an hour. Finely chop the onion and sauti it in hot oil, then add the garlic, celery, tomatoes, sugar and 1 cup of water. Boil the sauce for about half an hour. Strain the beans, spread them in a dish and add the sauce together with salt and pepper. Bake in the oven for about 40 minutes.

½ kg giant dried beans

1 onion

1-2 cloves of garlic

1 bunch of celery

2 tomatoes

1 tsp sugar

Salt, pepper

1 cup olive oil

Lentils

After washing the lentils well, boil them in a pan with water for 10 minutes. Strain off the liquid and add fresh water to cover. Add the finely chopped onion, puree, salt and pepper, bay leaf and oil. Leave to cook until the lentils have softened and the sauce has thickened.

½ kg lentils
2 tbs tomato puree
1 onion
1 bay leaf
Salt, pepper
1 cup olive oil

Lentils and rice

Place the lentils in a pan with just enough water to cover them and bring to the boil. Drain and add fresh water; as soon as the liquid boils again, add the rice and the salt and allow to cook. Gently fry the finely chopped onions and add them, with the oil, to the pan of rice and lentils. Stir well together and after a little while, when the mixture has thickened, remove it from the heat.

1 cup lentils
½ cup rice
2 medium onions
Salt
1 cup olive oil

Chickpeas

Soak the chickpeas in water overnight to soften them. Next day, drain them, sprinkle over the baking soda, shake well to mix and leave them for half an hour. Then rinse them with abundant warm water and put them in a pan with water to boil, along with the oil, whole onion, salt and pepper. Leave over a low heat until they are left together with the oil. Shortly before removing them from the heat, add the lemon juice and the flour and let them boil a couple of times.

½ kg chickpeas
1 lemon
½ tsp baking soda
1 tbs flour
1 onion
Salt, pepper
1 cup olive oil

Chickpea fritters

Soak the chickpeas in water overnight to soften them. Next day, drain them, sprinkle over the baking soda, shake well to mix and leave them for half an hour. Then rinse them with abundant warm water and put them in a pan with water to boil, along with the oil, whole onion, salt and pepper, until they are very soft. Remove from the heat, strain them and mash them to a puree. Add to this the flour, onions, garlic and finely chopped dill, form the mixture into fritters and fry in very hot oil.

1 1/2 cups chickpeas
1/2 cup flour
4 fresh spring onions
3 cloves of garlic
1 bunch of dill
1 tsp baking soda
Salt, pepper
Oil for frying

Black-eyed beans with fennel

Boil the beans in water for about half and hour. Remove from the heat and strain. Pass the tomatoes through a sieve, cut up the fennel and the onion. Gently heat the oil and sautı the onion and the fennel. Add the sieved tomatoes and 2 cups of water, allow to boil and then simmer for about 20 minutes. Finally, add the beans and a little more water, if needed, and cook over a moderate heat.

½ kg black-eyed beans

½ kg tomatoes

1 bunch fennel

1 onion

1 cup olive oil

Salt and pepper

Dried broad beans

Soak the dried broad beans in water overnight to soften them. Next day, rinse them and boil for about half an hour. Remove from the heat and strain. When they are cooled, remove the skins and throw them into a pan containing 2 cups of water and salt. When they have softened and absorbed the water, remove them from the heat. Pour over fresh olive oil and serve garnished with finely chopped spring onion.

½ kg dried broad beans

1 onion

1 cup olive oil

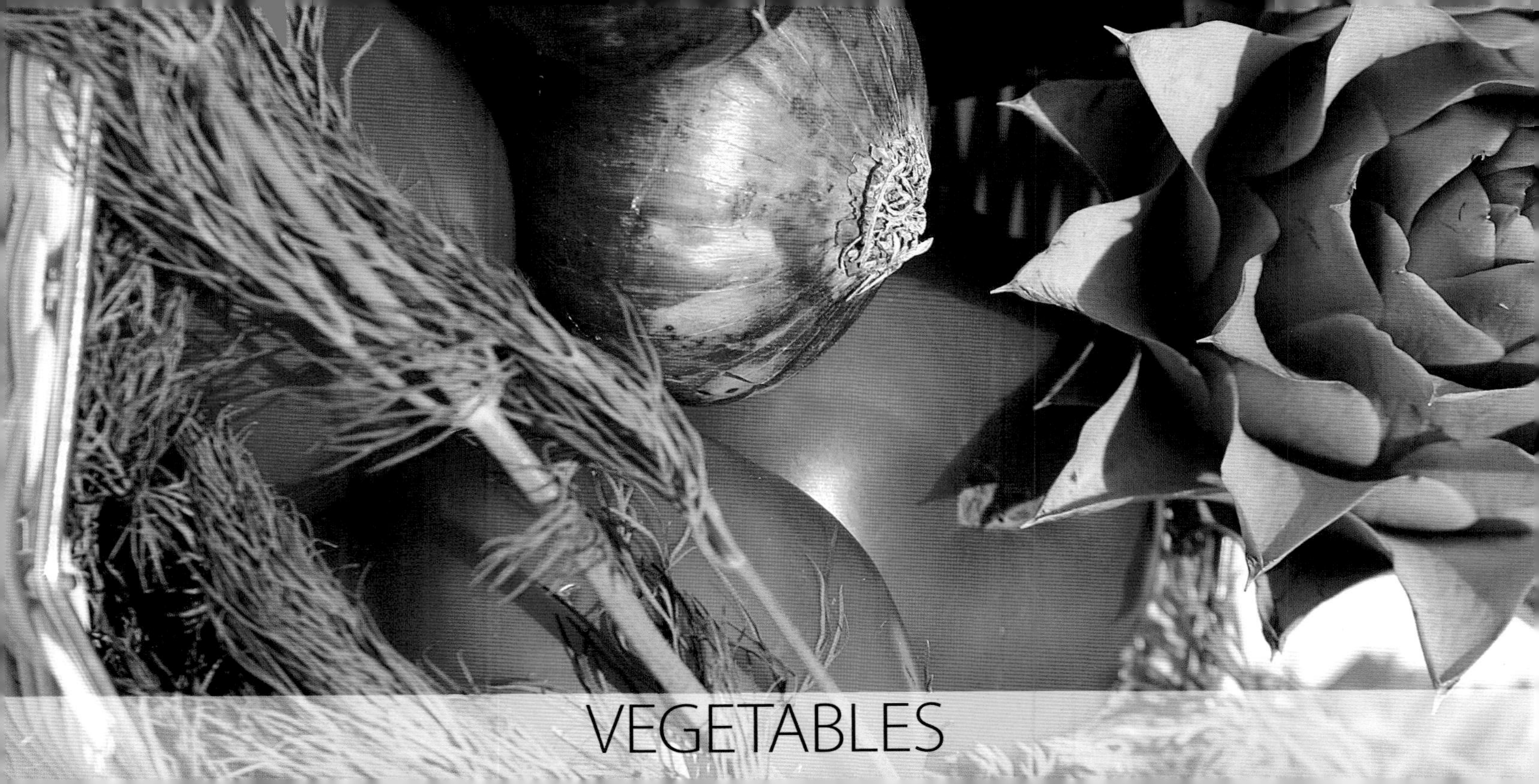

VEGETABLES

Beetroots

Beetroots

Oil

Vinegar

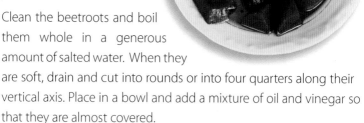

Clean the beetroots and boil them whole in a generous amount of salted water. When they are soft, drain and cut into rounds or into four quarters along their vertical axis. Place in a bowl and add a mixture of oil and vinegar so that they are almost covered.

Green beans

Prepare the beans and wash them well. Sauté the onion and then add the beans. Add the chopped tomatoes, salt and pepper, and 1 cup of water. Leave to simmer over a medium heat for about 45 minutes. If liked, add two potatoes, cut into medium slices, after about 20 minutes.

1 kg fresh green beans

½ kg tomatoes

1 onion

1 cup olive oil

1-2 potatoes (optional)

Salt, pepper

Okra

Prepare the okra, wash and drain them, then sprinkle them with vinegar and salt. Heat the oil in a pan and sauté the onion; before it begins to brown, add the chopped tomatoes and the pepper. When the sauce begins to boil, add the okra and, if necessary, a little water. Cook for about 30 minutes.

1 kg okra
1 cup oil
1 medium onion
2-3 tomatoes
Vinegar
Salt and pepper

Stuffed vegetables

Blanch the vine leaves, and wash and finely chop the herbs. Carefully scoop out the centres of the tomatoes, potatoes, aubergines and courgettes, leaving only the shell. Put the contents of the tomatoes into a bowl, to use in the filling. Add to this the finely chopped herbs, the grated onion, the rice, ½ cup of oil, a little of the water from the vine leaves and salt. Place the shells of the vegetables in a dish and fill them with the mixture, taking care that they are not filled to the top (otherwise the rice will expand and then overflow). Carefully roll up the same mixture in the vine leaves, so that it cannot escape from the edges, and also use it to stuff the courgette flowers. If there is any mixture left over add it around the vegetables, pour in the remainder of the oil and water, and bake in the oven.

800 gr rice for the filling

300 gr vine leaves

5 ripe tomatoes

5 peppers

5 courgettes

3 round aubergines

3 round potatoes

10 courgette flowers

3 onions

A few mint leaves

1 bunch parsley

1 bunch dill

2 cups oil

Salt, pepper

Stuffed courgette flowers

Carefully wash the flowers and cut out the stigma from the centre. Finely chop the onions, the garlic, dill, parsley and mint and put them in a bowl with the rice and oil. Season well. With a small spoon, fill the flowers with the mixture, taking care that the mixture does not come right to the top. Close the flowers and place them in a pan with the closed side downwards. Cover the flowers with an inverted plate, to keep them immobile while they are simmering. Add enough water to cover and cook for half an hour until the rice has absorbed the water and only the flowers with their oil remain.

20 courgette flowers
½ kg rice for filling
5 onions
2-3 cloves of garlic
1 bunch dill
1 bunch parsley
A few mint leaves
Salt, pepper
1 cup olive oil

'Volvi' (askordoulaki)

Clean the 'volvi' in the same way as onions, wash them well and cut a cross into the base of each. Boil in copious water. Change the water 2 or 3 times, in order to remove their bitterness. Add the salt to the final boiling. When they are ready, drain and serve them sprinkled with a mixture of oil and vinegar, and scatter over some finely chopped garlic and dill.

1 kg 'volvi'
5 tbs olive oil
100 gr vinegar
Salt
Garlic
Dill

Briam

Prepare the vegetables and wash them well; cut them into slices, season with salt and spread them out in a baking dish. Finely chop the onions, garlic, parsley and tomatoes. Season and add to the dish. Add the oil and one cup of water. If liked, scatter over pieces of feta or another salty cheese. Bake in a moderate oven for about one hour.

3 aubergines

4-5 courgettes

4-5 tomatoes

2 onions

2 cloves of garlic

2 green peppers

Finely chopped parsley

2 cups olive oil

Salt, pepper

Salty cheese (optional)

Artichokes with yogurt

Prepare and wash the artichokes and place them in a bowl to which the juice of the lemon and the flour have been added. Sauti the onion in the oil and carefully add the artichokes. Add the salt, pepper and enough water to cover. Simmer for 15-20 minutes and then add the yogurt. Allow to come to the boil once or twice, for the sauce to bind, and then turn off the heat.

2 kg cleaned and prepared artichokes

1 kg yogurt

1 onion

1 cup olive oil

1 lemon

1 tbs flour

Salt, pepper

Courgette fritters

Wash the courgettes and grate them; sprinkle with salt and leave to drain. Then place them in a bowl with the crumbled feta cheese, breadcrumbs, beaten eggs, finely chopped parsley and pepper. Mix to a paste and then form into round fritters. Dip in flour and fry in very hot oil.

1 kg courgettes
1 cup flour
1 cup breadcrumbs
250 gr feta cheese
2 eggs
Parsley
Salt and pepper
Olive oil for frying

Spinach rice

Prepare and wash the spinach. Sautı the finely chopped onion in very hot oil and then add the dill and spinach, cooking it until it wilts. Add 1 cup of water and as soon as the mixture comes to the boil, add the rice; season well and allow to cook. Then remove from the heat and serve hot with lemon.

1 kg spinach
1 cup rice
1 onion
1 bunch of dill
Salt, pepper
1 cup olive oil

Cabbage rice

Bring the oil to a high temperature in a pan and sautı the finely chopped onion. Shred the cabbage and add to the onion in the pan, stir well and then add 1 cup of water and the lemon juice. When the mixture boils, add the rice and one more cup of water. Season well, reduce the heat and leave to boil for about 15 minutes, until a thickish sauce remains.

1 medium-sized cabbage
1 onion
1/2 cup rice
Juice of 1 lemon
Salt, pepper
1/2 cup olive oil

Cauliflower with spinach

Wash the leeks and cut them into medium-sized pieces. Pour the oil into a saucepan and gently sautı the leeks in it with the finely chopped onion. Add the wine and a little water. Meanwhile, wash the spinach and cut it into largish pieces; when the leeks are half-cooked, add the spinach to the pan along with the tomato puree. At the same time, bring the cauliflower, cut into florets, to the boil in water in another pan. Then add it to the pan with the spinach and allow the food to cook until only the vegetables and a thickish sauce remain.

½ kg cauliflower

½ kg spinach

3 leeks

1 bunch of dill or fennel

1 cup of oil

1 onion

½ cup red wine

1 level tbs tomato puree

Salt, pepper

Aubergine rice with mint

Wash the aubergines, cut them into medium-sized cubes, sprinkle with salt and leave for an hour to sweeten. Put the oil into a pan and sautı the finely chopped onion. Add the aubergines, mix well and leave to cook on a low heat for 5 minutes. Add the finely chopped tomatoes or puree to the pan and after another five minutes, add 4 cups of water. As soon as the water begins to boil add the rice, mix well and leave to simmer for about 15 minutes. When it is ready, add the mint, turn off the heat and cover the pan with a clean tea towel for a short time, until the mint leaves have wilted.

1 kg elongated aubergines

1 ½ cups of rice

1 onion

2 tomatoes or 1 tbs puree

1 soup spoon fresh mint

1 cup olive oil

Salt, pepper

Courgette 'boreki'

Prepare and wash the vegetables. Cut the potatoes and courgettes into rounds with a thickness of about 1 cm and place them in separate bowls. Mash the cheese. Chop the tomatoes and add to the courgettes along with the finely chopped mint, salt and pepper, and mix well. Spread half of the potatoes in an oiled dish and then add a total of three alternating layers of the cheese and the courgette mixture. Finally, scatter over the remaining potatoes and sprinkle them with oregano. Pour over the oil and place in a preheated oven. Bake for about one hour, at first at a high temperature, and then reduce to a lower one.

½ kg courgettes
½ kg potatoes
2 large tomatoes
400 gr myzithra cheese
½ cup olive oil
A few mint leaves
½ tsp oregano
Salt and pepper

Little onion pies

Peel the potatoes and the onions and pass them through a mincer. Add the eggs, the flour, the finely chopped mint, the salt and pepper and mix well together. Pour the oil into a frying pan and heat well. Drop small amounts of the mixture into the pan with a spoon and fry them, taking care to brown them on both sides.

½ kg potatoes
½ kg onions
2 eggs
1½ cups flour
A few mint leaves
Salt, pepper

Artichokes with broad beans

Remove the leaves and the choke and only leave the heads of the artichokes. Cut them into halves and throw them into a bowl containing water mixed with 1 tbs of the flour and the juice of 1 lemon. Then prepare the broad beans, retaining mostly the beans themselves but also some parts of the pods. Cut the onions into small pieces and sautı them in warmed oil and then add the artichokes, beans, dill, salt, pepper and two cups of water. Bring to the boil, add the remaining flour dissolved in the juice of one lemon and leave to cook over a low heat for about one hour.

8-10 artichokes
1 kg broad beans
1 bunch of dill
1 bunch of fresh spring onions
2 lemons
2 tbs flour
1 cup olive oil

Oven-baked potatoes

Wash and peel the potatoes and cut them into medium-sized pieces. If they are very small, leave them whole and simply make a cut in them so that they roast better. Spread them out in a dish and season with salt, pepper and oregano. Add the oil, the lemon juice and 2 cups of water and shake the dish well so that the oil and seasonings are evenly distributed . Bake in the oven for about 1 hour.

1 kg potatoes
Juice of 1 lemon
Oregano
Salt, pepper
1 cup olive oil

Potatoes boiled with wild greens

1 kg wild greens (various types)

½ kg potatoes

3 onions

1 tsp tomato puree (optional)

1 cup olive oil

Pick over the greens, wash them and cut them into thick sections. Place in a pan together with the finely chopped onion and the oil. Cover the pan and set the heat to low. As soon as the greens wilt and reduce in volume, add 1 cup of water and stir well. Bring them to the boil and then add the potatoes cut into small pieces, or whole if they are small. Season with salt and pepper, and if liked, add the tomato puree. Cook over a moderate heat, until only a little sauce remains.

Fried aubergines with a red sauce

Wash the aubergines and cut them into slices, sprinkle with salt and leave them for about half an hour. Rinse them, drain well and then fry them. In another pan heat the oil, sauti the garlic and add the chopped tomatoes. Season with salt and pepper, add one cup of water and leave the sauce to simmer until it thickens. Place the fried aubergines in a dish, pour over the tomato sauce and bake in the oven for about 15-20 minutes.

1 kg aubergines

4-5 ripe tomatoes

4 cloves of garlic, finely chopped

Salt and pepper

½ cup olive oil

Potatoes with chestnuts

Sauti the chestnuts and the finely chopped onion in the oil, then add the tomato, also chopped, salt, pepper and one cup of water. Finally, throw in the potatoes and leave to cook until the potatoes have softened and a thickish sauce remains.

Chestnuts roasted in the oven or over a fire

1 tomato

2 onions

3-4 potatoes

Salt, pepper

1 cup olive oil

Aubergines Imam

Cut off the top of the aubergines, score them lengthwise, salt them and leave to drain for about 30 minutes. Rinse them, then cut them in half and fry them in very hot oil. When the flesh has softened, remove the aubergines from the pan with a slotted spoon and without breaking the skins scoop out the flesh with a spoon, keeping it separate. Gently sautı the onions in a pan with the garlic, cut into slices. Add the remaining ingredients (and the flesh of the aubergines) and allow them to soften. Place the aubergines in a dish and fill them with the mixture from the pan. If any filling is left over, pour it over the dish. Add a little oil and 1 cup of water and place the dish in a moderate oven for about half an hour.

4 aubergines

2 tomatoes

3 onions

4 cloves of garlic

½ bunch of parsley

Salt, pepper

1 cup olive oil

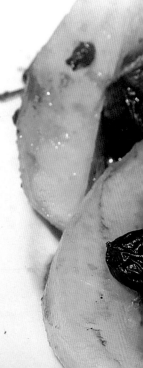

Fried aubergines

1 kg round aubergines
3-4 tbs flour
Salt
Grated cheese
Beer
Oil for frying

Wash the aubergines and cut them into rounds. Dip them one by one into a bowl containing beer. Drain well, season with salt and coat with flour. Heat olive oil in a frying pan to a high temperature and fry the aubergines. As soon as they are ready arrange the slices on a plate and scatter grated cheese over them.

Aubergine rolls with cheese

Cut the stalks off the aubergines, wash them and cut into slices. Place them in a bowl of water to sweeten. Meanwhile, prepare the sauce: sautı the onion in the oil, add the pureed tomatoes, salt, pepper and thyme and leave the sauce to cook. Drain the aubergines well, brush them with oil on the inside and spread 1 tsp of the crumbled feta on each. Roll them up and fasten with a toothpick to secure the ends. Arrange them in a dish, pour over the sauce and bake in the oven for about half and hour.

4 bottle-shaped aubergines

1 kg tomatoes

1 large onion

500 gr feta cheese

1 ½ cups olive oil

Salt, pepper, thyme

Leeks with spinach

Wash the leeks well and cut into medium-sized slices. Put them into a pan with the oil (no water) and leave them over a low heat until they soften. Peel the potatoes and cut them into medium-sized pieces. Add them to the pan containing the leeks with the puree and a little water, if needed. Cook until the potatoes are well done and a thickish sauce is left with the vegetables.

1 kg leeks

1 kg spinach

1 bunch spring onions

1 bunch dill or fennel

2-3 potatoes

1 level tbs tomato puree

1½ cups oil

Salt, pepper

Boiled wild greens

Pick over the greens, chop them and wash very carefully. Place a pan containing a generous amount of water on the heat and when it boils, add the greens. After about 20 minutes they will be cooked. Strain, season and serve hot or cold with lemon, salt, and a generous quantity of olive oil.

1 kg wild greens

Salt

Lemon

Olive oil

Mushroom stew

Wash the mushrooms, cut off the stems and score them. Drain them, press out the water and if they are large cut them into smaller sections. Pour the oil into a pan and sautı the finely chopped onion together with the mushrooms. Add the chopped tomatoes, rosemary, salt and pepper. Cover and leave to cook over a low heat for about one hour. Meanwhile, prepare the small onions; sautı them in a little oil, pour over the wine and add the contents of the pan to the mushrooms. Allow to simmer for about half an hour. Before turning off the heat, check to see if the mushrooms are still tough – if so, cook for a little longer.

1 kg flat mushrooms

1 large onion

1/2 kg small stewing onions

1/2 kg ripe tomatoes

1 cup red wine

1 cup olive oil

1/2 cup rosemary

Salt, pepper

Tomato soup

Boil together the tomato juice and the water for about 10 minutes. Add the oil, rice, salt and pepper. When the rice has softened add the parsley and bring to the boil once or twice again.

2 cups tomato juice

1 cup rice

4 cups water

1/2 cup olive oil

Finely chopped parsley

Salt, pepper

Avronies

Wash the avronies, cut them in pieces, separating the stems from the tips, and plunge them into boiling water. Pour the oil into a pan and sautı the finely chopped onions. Add the stems of the avronies with a little water. As soon as they are half cooked, add the tips and season well; continue cooking them. When they are ready add 1 tsp of flour dissolved in a little water and vinegar (as much as you like). Stir everything together and as soon as the sauce thickens remove the pan from the heat.

1 kg avronies (thin wild asparagus)

3 large onions

1 cup oil

1 tbs flour

Vinegar

Salt, pepper

Rabbit 'youvetsi'

Wash the rabbit and cut it into pieces. Heat the oil to a high temperature in a pan and stew the onions together with the rabbit, stirring constantly. Add the tomatoes, salt and pepper and 2 cups of water, and bring to the boil. When the meat is half-cooked, transfer it to a dish or better still, a clay pot (youvetsi). Scatter over the pasta grains, add 2 cups of hot water and bake in the oven for 30-40 minutes.

1 rabbit
1/2 kg fine pasta grains
3-4 ripe tomatoes
1 onion
Cinnamon
Salt, pepper
1 cup olive oil

Rabbit in wine

A few hours beforehand, or better still the day before, prepare a marinade by mixing the wine, onions and garlic finely chopped, bay leaf, thyme, pepper and clove. Add the rabbit, cut into sections. When the time comes to cook, drain the rabbit and toss in flour; heat the oil and brown it carefully. Add the marinade and 1 cup of water and allow all to simmer for about 1- 1 ½ hours.

1 rabbit
2 cups red wine
2 onions
1 clove of garlic
1 twig of thyme
1 bay leaf
1 clove
2 tbs flour
Salt, pepper
1 cup olive oil

Rabbit in a red sauce

Wash the rabbit, cut it into pieces and leave to drain. Heat the oil to a high temperature in a pan and immediately sautı the finely chopped onion with the meat. Add the wine and then the chopped tomatoes, salt, pepper and a cup of water. Reduce the heat and leave the meat to simmer. Check periodically and, if necessary, add more water. When the meat is tender and the sauce has thickened, turn off the heat. Serve the dish with fried potatoes.

1 rabbit

1 onion

3-4 ripe tomatoes

1 cup oil

½ cup red wine

Salt, pepper

Rabbit or hare stew

1 hare or 1 rabbit, 2.5 - 3 kg in weight

3 kg small onions

2-3 bay leaves

1 deep plateful of chopped tomatoes

2 cloves of garlic

A few cloves

1 glass red wine

1 cup olive oil

Salt, pepper

Wash the rabbit or hare and cut it into pieces. Prepare the onions and push a clove into some of them. Sautι the meat in very hot oil and add the onions. Cover the pan for a few minutes, then remove the lid and add 1 wineglass of red wine. Add the tomatoes, bay leaves, salt and pepper and 2 cups of water. Allow to simmer over a low heat for about one hour. Serve with fried potatoes.

Rabbit with yogurt

Wash and drain the rabbit. Season well. Beat together the yogurt with the butter and fill the stomach cavity of the rabbit with it. Sew the stomach up tightly so that the mixture cannot ooze out. Brush the rabbit with oil and place in the oven. Roast for about 2 hours in a moderate oven, taking care to turn the rabbit occasionally so that it roasts from all sides.

1 rabbit

½ kg yogurt

100 gr butter

Salt, pepper

Rabbit with artichokes

Wash, drain and cut up the rabbit. Heat the oil in a pan and add the meat. Brown on all sides, turning frequently, and 'quench' with the red wine. Add the whole small onions, season, and then add a glass of water. Cover and leave to cook over a medium heat. Now clean and prepare the artichokes, leaving them whole if they are small and incising a cross into the base, or cutting them into two pieces if large. To prevent them from discolouring, place them in a bowl of water containing the juice of one lemon. About 15 minutes before the end of the roasting time, add the artichokes to the rabbit. As soon as they have softened, remove a little of the juices from the pan to a small bowl. Add the juice from the lemons, the flour and the water. Beat well and then pour the mixture into the pan and shake well to distribute the liquid. Allow the sauce to boil and as soon as it has thickened, remove from the heat.

1 medium-sized rabbit

10-12 artichokes

4 small onions

3 lemons

1 glass red wine

1 tbs flour

1 cup oil

Salt, pepper

Lemon chicken with potatoes

Wash the chicken and cut into portions. Sautı the pieces in hot oil and then add the lemon juice, potatoes, oregano, salt, pepper and 2 cups of water. Leave to simmer over a low heat for about 1 hour.

1 chicken

2 kg small potatoes

1/2 glass lemon juice

oregano

salt, pepper

1 cup olive oil

Rooster with 'hylopites'

Wash the bird, cut into pieces and sautı in a little oil. As soon as it begins to brown, add the onion and stir together. Add the wine, salt, pepper, fresh tomatoes, oil and a little water. Allow to simmer until the meat is tender. Remove the meat from the pan, add the hylopites and boil in the liquid for about 15 minutes. Put the meat into a baking dish or clay pot, add the hylopites and the sun-dried tomatoes and cook in a moderate oven for about another 30 minutes. As soon as it is removed from the oven, sprinkle over the grated cheese.

500 gr hylopites

1 rooster, about 1 1/2 kg in weight

1 cup olive oil

1 finely chopped onion

2 cups chopped tomatoes

10 sun-dried tomatoes

1/2 cup red wine

Salt, pepper

Grated kefalotyri cheese

Chicken with peppers

Fry the chicken in the oil, having first tossed the pieces in a mixture of flour, salt, pepper and paprika. Remove the chicken with a slotted spoon and in the same oil sautı the onion, garlic, and peppers cut into small pieces. As soon as they have softened, add the tomato juice and leave the sauce to cook for a short time over a low heat. Now add the chicken, cover the pan and cook for about another thirty minutes.

1 chicken cut into portions

1 onion

1 clove of garlic

3 green peppers

3 red peppers

1 cup tomato juice

1 cup oil

1 cup flour

Salt, pepper, paprika

Chicken with piquant olives

Wash the chicken well, cut into portions, sprinkle with salt and leave to drain. Bring the oil to a high temperature in a pan and sautı the meat with the onions and garlic. 'Quench' with the wine and add the chopped tomatoes, oregano, pepper, a pinch of salt and 2 cups of water. Leave to cook for about 45 minutes and then add the olives from which you have removed the stones. Cook for a further 15 minutes.

1 ½ kg chicken

4-5 ripe tomatoes

150 gr black olives preserved in vinegar

10 small onions

1 clove of garlic

1 cup wine

Oregano

1 cup oil

Salt, pepper

Chicken pilaf

1 free-range chicken
Rice for pilaf
1 lemon
Salt, pepper

Wash the chicken, cut into pieces and put in a pan to boil with a good quantity of water. Remove the scum from the initial boiling with a slotted spoon. Now add salt and leave to simmer until the meat is tender. Strain the liquid through a fine sieve and retain the meat separately. Put the liquid back into the pan, measuring it in cups so that the amount of rice to be used can be calculated. The proportion should be 3 parts of liquid to one part of rice. As soon as the liquid has boiled again, add the rice and leave over a low heat, stirring occasionally. When the rice has swollen and absorbed the liquid, turn off the heat and add a few drops of lemon juice.

Chicken in a red sauce

Wash the chicken and cut into pieces; leave to drain. Pour the oil into a pan and as soon as it is hot, sautı the finely chopped onion and the meat. When it has browned add the tomatoes, crushed, the sugar, salt, pepper and one cup of water. Reduce the heat and leave to simmer gently until the meat is tender and left with a thickish sauce. This dish can be served with fried potatoes, rice or macaroni.

1 chicken
½ cup oil
4-5 ripe tomatoes
1 onion
1 tsp sugar
salt, pepper

'Coq au vin'

Wash the bird and cut into pieces. Sautı the finely chopped onion, garlic, and meat in hot oil. After a few minutes, 'quench' the meat with the wine and add the chopped tomatoes, salt, pepper and 2 cups of water. Leave to simmer over a low heat for about 1 hour. Serve with fried potatoes or rice.

1 rooster or chicken

1 onion

2 cloves of garlic

1 deep plate of chopped tomatoes

1 glass red wine

Salt, pepper

1 cup olive oil

Chicken with yogurt

Wash the chicken and cut into pieces, pour over the lemon juice and season, and leave in a bowl for 1 hour. Then place in a baking dish with the oil and a little water and bake in the oven. Beat the yogurt with the eggs and 2 tbs of water and when the chicken is ready, pour over the sauce. Return the dish to the oven for a short time, and then it is ready.

1 ½ kg chicken
½ kg yogurt
1 cup oil
2 lemons
2 eggs
Salt, pepper
A few breadcrumbs

Chicken with okra

Wash the chicken, cut it into pieces and leave to drain. Pour the oil into a pan and sauti the finely chopped onions with the meat. As soon as it has browned, add the chopped tomatoes, sugar, salt, pepper and 1 cup of water. Reduce the heat and leave to simmer. When the meat is tender remove it from the pan with a slotted spoon and arrange it on a plate. Now wash the okra, removing their caps, and fry them gently in very hot oil, in stages, until they brown. Then put them into the pan containing the sauce from the meat, add a little water and leave to cook over a low heat. Do not stir, as this would break up the okra. When they are ready, add them to the plate containing the chicken and pour any remaining sauce over the whole dish.

1 chicken

1 kg okra

½ cup oil

1 kg ripe tomatoes

2 onions

1 tsp sugar

Salt, pepper

Beef in a red sauce

Wash the beef and cut it into small pieces. Gently fry the finely chopped onion, garlic and meat in hot oil for a few minutes, then pour over the wine and add the tomato, bay leaf, clove, cinnamon, salt, pepper and 2 cups of water. Allow to simmer over a low heat for about 1 hour. Serve with fried potatoes, rice or boiled pasta.

1 kg beef

1 onion

2 cloves of garlic

1 kg chopped tomatoes

1-2 bay leaves

1 cinnamon stick

3-4 cloves

1 glass red wine

Salt, pepper

1 cup olive oil

Beef with macaroni

Wash the meat, cut it into pieces and leave for a while to drain. Heat the oil in a pan and sautı the finely chopped onion and the meat. As soon as the latter begins to brown, add the finely chopped tomatoes, salt, pepper, and 2 cups of water. Leave to simmer and shortly before it is ready add another 4 cups of water. When the liquid boils, add the macaroni and leave to cook until it is soft and there is only a little red sauce left in the pan.

1 kg beef
1/2 cup oil
1 onion
3-4 ripe tomatoes
1/2 kg macaroni
Salt, pepper

Beef with courgettes, egg and lemon

Cut the meat into medium-sized pieces, wash it and leave to drain. Heat the oil to a very high temperature in a pan and gently fry the meat to brown it on all sides. Add the onions and continue to fry everything together. Add 2 cups of water, salt, and pepper, cover the pan and leave the meat to cook over a low temperature. In the meantime, wash the courgettes and cut them into large pieces (leave whole if very small), and finely chop the dill. When the meat is half cooked, add the courgettes and dill to the pan. When everything is ready, turn off the heat and prepare the egg and lemon sauce as follows: beat the eggs well and without stopping, add the juice of the lemons and a little of the juices from the pan. Then pour the sauce over the meat and courgettes, shaking the pan so that it is well distributed, and serve.

1 kg beef
1 onion
1 cup oil
1 kg courgettes
1 bunch of dill
2 eggs
2 lemons
Salt, pepper

Beef with peas

Cut the meat into medium-sized pieces, wash and leave it to strain. Heat the oil to a very high temperature in a pan and gently fry the meat to brown it on all sides. Add the onions and continue to fry everything together. Add the chopped tomatoes, salt, and pepper, cover the pan and reduce the heat. When the meat is partly cooked, add the peas and a little water and leave to cook further until the meat is tender and the sauce thick.

1 kg beef
1kg peas
1 cup oil
1 onion
4-5 ripe tomatoes
1 bunch of dill
Salt, pepper

Beef in wine sauce

Cut the meat into cubes. Wash the vegetables well and cut them, with the onions, into large pieces. Heat the oil well in a pan and first fry the vegetables and then the meat. When it is browned on all sides add the chopped tomatoes, wine, bay leaves, salt and pepper. Transfer the contents of the pan to a baking tin or oven glass dish and bake in the oven for about 1 ½ hours.

½ kg beef
3-4 ripe tomatoes
3 small onions
1 cup red wine
2-3 bay leaves
½ cup olive oil
Salt, pepper

Beef with peppers

1 kg beef
4-5 ripe tomatoes
1 kg peppers
½ kg onions
Salt, pepper
1 cup olive oil

Heat the oil well in a pan and fry the meat, which you have cut into cubes. When it is browned on all sides add the chopped onion, peppers cut into thick pieces, chopped tomatoes, salt and pepper. Sauti well together and add 2 cups of water. Leave to simmer over a low heat until a thickish sauce remains.

Beef with green olives

Wash the meat and cut into medium-sized pieces. Heat the oil in a pan and fry the meat until it browns. Add the chopped tomatoes, finely chopped garlic, cinnamon, salt and pepper and 1 cup of water. Leave to simmer for about 20 minutes. In the meantime, toss the green olives into scalding hot water and when the meat is half cooked, add them to the pan. Cook for about another half an hour.

1 kg beef
½ kg green olives
3-4 ripe tomatoes
1 clove of garlic
Cinnamon
Salt, pepper
1 cup olive oil

Beef with quinces

Finely chop the onions and sautı them in half of the oil together with the meat cut into small pieces. Add 2 cups of water, the tomato paste, sugar, salt and pepper and leave to cook over a low heat for about half an hour. In the meantime wash the quinces, cut into thick slices and sautı them in a frying pan with a little oil. When the meat is almost cooked, transfer it to a baking dish, add the quinces, cinnamon and bay leaf, and place it in the oven to bake for a while.

1 kg beef

1 kg quinces

1 onion

3 tbs tomato paste

1 tsp sugar

1 bay leaf

1 cinnamon stick

Salt, pepper

1 cup olive oil

Lamb with okra

Wash the okra and lightly cut into their caps. Cut the meat into portions and sauti it in hot oil together with the finely chopped onion. Add the juice from the tomatoes to the pan and bring to the boil. Now add the okra, salt, pepper and 2 cups of water, and leave to cook over a low heat.

1 kg lamb
1 kg okra
½ kg tomatoes
1 onion
Salt, pepper
1 cup oil

Lamb youvetsi

Wash the meat, cut it into portions and place it in a baking dish. Add the tomatoes, onions and the finely chopped garlic, salt, pepper, oil and 1 cup of water. Bake in the oven and when the meat is almost cooked, add the 'kritharaki'.

1 kg lamb
½ kg 'kritharaki' (grain-sized pasta)
½ kg tomatoes
1 onion
1 whole garlic
1 cup olive oil
Salt, pepper

Lamb with courgettes

Wash the meat, cut into pieces, season it and roll in flour. Heat the oil in a pan and sautı the finely chopped onion together with the meat. Add the chopped tomatoes, finely chopped parsley, salt, pepper and 2 cups of water. Cover the pan and leave to cook for one hour. In the meantime wash the courgettes; cut them into medium-sized pieces or if they are very small, they may be left whole. Add to the meat in the pan and continuing cooking for about another half hour.

1 kg lamb
1kg courgettes
3-4 ripe tomatoes
1 onion
Parsley
2-3 tbs flour
Salt, pepper
½ cup olive oil

Lamb with hylopites

Cut the meat into cubes and sautı in very hot oil wit the finely chopped onion and garlic. Add the pepper and carrot. After another 2 minutes, add I cup of water and as soon as it boils remove the scum that forms with a slotted spoon. Leave the meat to simmer for about 1 hour. When it is half cooked, add the chopped tomatoes and seasonings. Add the hylopites and continue to cook for about another 20 minutes until the red sauce has thickened, the hylopites are cooked and the meat is tender. Serve hot, sprinkled with the grated cheese.

1 kg lamb
1 onion
½ clove of garlic
4 tbs oil
1 pepper
1 carrot
2 medium-sized tomatoes
½ kg hylopites
½ cup grated cheese
Salt, pepper

Lamb fricasée

Wash the meat, season and cut into portions. Heat the oil in a pan, sauté the onions which have previously been cut into thick chunks, and add the meat. When the meat is well fried, add ½ cup of water and bring to the boil. Wash and pick over the parsley (or lettuce), add it to the meat in the pan and season with salt and pepper. When the dish is ready, beat the eggs and without stopping, gradually add the lemon juice as well as a little of the liquid from the pan. Now add the egg and lemon sauce to the pan, shaking it well to distribute evenly, and the food is ready.

Lamb fricasée can be made with parsley or lettuce – the method is the same.

1 kg lamb

½ kg small onions

1 kg parsley or 3 lettuces

2 eggs

1 lemon

½ cup oil

Salt, pepper

'Browned' lamb

Cut the meat into small pieces, wash and leave to drain well. Heat the oil in a pan and immediately add the meat, salt and pepper. When it begins to brown, reduce the heat, cover the pan and leave the meat to brown further in the oil (without water) until it is tender.

1 kg lamb

4 tbs oil

Salt, pepper

Lamb 'ofto' or 'antikristo'

Cut the meat into large pieces. Season well with salt, dust with oregano and thread the pieces onto canes cut from the stems of vines. Start a fire in the open air and place the canes in a circular pattern around the fire, some distance from it. Leave to roast for about two hours, remembering to turn the meat periodically, so that it roasts well from all sides.

1 lamb
Coarse salt
Oregano
Vine canes

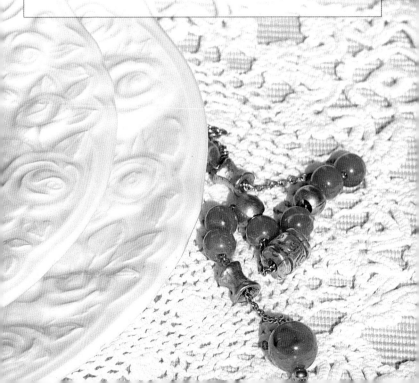

Lamb with stamnangathi, egg and lemon

Boil the stamnangathi in just enough water for about 10 minutes. Drain well and set aside. Wash the meat, cut into pieces, drain well and sauté in a pan with the oil. Lower the heat and leave to cook for about half an hour, without adding water. When it is partly cooked, add the stamnangathi, salt and pepper to the meat and cover the pan. Finally, when the food is just ready, prepare the egg and lemon by beating the egg and gradually adding the lemon juice. Take a little of the juices from the pan and beat them into the mixture gradually so that it does not curdle. Add to the pan and shake it to distribute the sauce. It is now ready to serve.

2 kg lamb

1 cup oil

1 1/2 kg stamnangathi (wild chicory)

1 egg

2 lemons

Salt, pepper

Lamb with cream, wrapped in fyllo

Wash the meat, cut it into small pieces and leave to drain. Meanwhile, beat the yogurt in a bowl with the cream, eggs and a little salt. Heat the oil to a high temperature in a pan and sauté the meat until it browns. Butter one piece of fyllo pastry, spread another on top and place a piece of meat which has been dunked in the cream mixture on top of it.

Add a little more of the mixture to it. Roll up the meat and filling carefully in the pastry, so that it does not escape from the sides, and place in a buttered baking dish. Continue thus until all the meat has been rolled up. When the dish is full, brush all the rolls with butter and bake in a moderate oven until they are browned.

1 ½ kg lean, boned lamb

¾ kg strained yogurt

200 gr cream

2 eggs

Salt, pepper

½ kg fyllo pastry

½ cup olive oil

A little butter

Lamb with yogurt

Wash the meat, season it with salt and leave it to marinate for one night in the refrigerator. Next day, wipe the meat, make some incisions into it and push slivers of garlic into them. Pour over the oil, scatter over pepper and thyme, and roast the lamb in the oven at 200 C. When it is ready, take the juices from the pan and beat them together with the yogurt and the beaten eggs. Remove the meat from the bone, and if liked, transfer it from the roasting tin to a more closed vessel, such as a clay pot. Pour over the yogurt sauce. Return the meat to the oven for about half an hour until the sauce has thickened and the yogurt has taken on a colour.

1 ½ kg leg of lamb

500 gr strained yogurt

2 eggs

1 lemon

2-3 cloves of garlic

½ cup oil

Thyme

Salt and pepper

Lamb with vegetables and yogurt

Wash the meat, cut into small pieces and drain well. Sauté the lamb in oil until it browns, add the wine, thyme, rosemary, salt and pepper and cook until half done. Meanwhile, cut the tomatoes and aubergines into slices, spread them out in an oiled dish and roast them in the oven for about 20 minutes. When they are ready, scatter the meat on top of them and pour over the yogurt into which you have mixed the cheese and eggs. Bake in the oven for about 1 hour.

1 kg lamb

1 kg tomatoes

1 kg aubergines

500 gr strained yogurt

250 gr graviera cheese

3 eggs

½ cup wine

½ cup oil

Thyme

Rosemary

Salt, pepper

Lamb with avronies

Cut up the meat, wash and drain it, and fry it in very hot oil until it is browned, adding the finely chopped onion towards the end. When the onion has softened, season well and add one cup of water. Cover the pan and leave to cook on a low heat. In the meantime, prepare, wash and cut up the avronies. When the meat is cooked, take it from the pan with a slotted spoon and set aside. Place the stalks of the avronies in the pan with a little water. When they are partly cooked add the tips, season and leave to cook further. Finally, dissolve 1 tbs of flour in the juice of 1 lemon, add it to the pan and shake to distribute it. Add the meat and bring all to the boil, when the sauce will thicken.

1 kg lamb
1 onion
1 kg avronies
1 lemon
Salt, pepper
2/3 cup oil

Lamb with pilaf (wedding pilaf)

1 kg lamb, from a larger (two-year old) animal

½ kg rice

Juice of two lemons

3-4 tbs stakovoutiro (thick, butter-like cream)

Salt

Wash the meat, cut it into pieces and boil in water with a little salt. When the meat is soft, remove it from the pan with a slotted spoon. Strain the liquid, so that it is clear, and return it to the pan along with the rice. The quantities needed for the traditional Cretan pilaf are 3 cups of liquid to 1 cup of rice. When the rice is cooked (after about 15 minutes) add the lemon juice and bring to the boil again. Turn off the heat, and add the softened stakovoutiro to the pilaf.

Lamb with artichokes, egg and lemon

Wash the meat, cut it into small pieces and leave to drain well. Heat the oil in a pan and sauté the finely chopped onions. Add the meat, mix together well and add the flour and enough water to cover the meat. Leave to simmer for about 1 hour. Meanwhile, prepare the artichokes and cut them into halves, rub them with lemon so that they do not discolour and place them in a bowl containing cold water. Wash and finely chop the onions and the dill. When the meat has softened add the artichokes and herbs to the pan, season, cover the pan and leave to cook for about another half hour. When it is ready, prepare the egg and lemon: beat the eggs and without stopping gradually add the lemon juice. Take a little of the sauce from the pan and continue to beat while adding it to the mixture. Finally, pour it over the meat in the pan and shake to distribute evenly; the dish is ready.

In many parts of Crete a chicken is boiled together with the lamb, in order to enrich the broth. The cooking method is the same.

1 kg lamb
1/2 cup oil
10-15 artichokes
1 onion
1 bunch of spring onions
1 bunch of dill
1 tbs flour
Salt, pepper
2 eggs
2 lemons

Lamb with potatoes in oven

Wash the meat and cut it into portions. If you have a leg of lamb, leave it whole, making a few cuts into it so that it will roast better. Brush with oil and place in a baking dish. Now peel the potatoes, which should preferably be small ones so that they can be left whole. If they are large, however, cut them into moderately sized pieces and make some slits in them. Put them in the dish around the meat, add the salt and pepper, thyme, lemon juice and the remaining oil and roast in a moderate oven for about 2 hours.

1 kg lamb
½ kg potatoes
Juice of 1 lemon
Thyme
Salt, pepper
½ cup olive oil

Pork with wild greens

1 kg pork
½ kg wild greens
2-3 onions
Salt, pepper
1 cup olive oil

Pick over and wash the greens well. Wash and cut the meat into portions. Bring the oil to a high temperature in a pan and add the meat. Allow to cook until half done, and meanwhile cut the greens into small pieces and finely chop the onions. Add to the pan with the meat, season, and cover the pan. Lower the heat and leave the meat to cook in the juices which are drawn out from the greens.

Pork with leeks

Cut the pork into medium-sized pieces, wash and leave it to drain. Put the oil into a pan and sauté the finely chopped onion with the meat. As soon as it brown, 'quench' it with the wine, add 1-2 cups of water and leave to cook over a low heat. Shortly before it is completely cooked, add the leeks, which have been washed and cut into medium-sized pieces. Season and leave to cook until a thickish sauce remains with the meat.

1 kg pork
1 kg leeks
1 onion
½ cup oil
½ cup white wine
Salt, pepper

Pork with celery

Cut the meat into portions, season and place in a pan with water to boil. When it has partly cooked, add the oil, finely chopped onion and the celery, which has been washed and cut into pieces about 5 cms in length. Leave to simmer for about 1 hour.

1 kg pork
1½ kg celery
2-3 onions
2 lemons
Salt, pepper
1 cup olive oil

Smoked pork

Cut the pork into elongated strips and wash them well. Place them in a container full of vinegar and leave them for 2-3 days. Then season well and hang them about half a metre directly above the place where you are going to light the fire. Try to make the fire from twigs of sage, bay or another Cretan aromatic plant, so that the meat will absorb their aroma and be even more delicious. Cover the fire with ash so that it smokes constantly, and leave the meat hanging over it, to cook and brown in the smoke. This is an excellent appetizer to serve with wine and can be kept for a number of days.

Lean pork, without fat

Vinegar

Salt, pepper

Pork with chickpeas

1 kg pork
1 onion
4-5 ripe tomatoes
½ kg chickpeas
1 cup oil
Salt, pepper

The evening before you intend to make the dish, place the chickpeas in a bowl of water and leave them overnight to soften.

Cut the meat into small portions, wash it and leave it to drain. Heat the oil in a pan and then sauté the meat and the finely chopped onion together until they brown. Add the tomatoes, also finely chopped, salt, pepper and a little water, and leave the meat to simmer for 10 minutes. Now add the chickpeas and enough water to cover, and leave the dish to simmer until the meat is well done and is left with its sauce.

'Omathies' (sausages)

Select the thickest of the pigs' intestines and wash them very well. Leave them for 2-3 days in a bowl containing water and the sliced lemons and bitter oranges. Ensure that the intestines are filled with this aromatized water, so that they are well cleaned and any odour removed. Change the water every day. Mix together the grain with the raisins, pepper, cinnamon and almonds or walnuts, which have been finely chopped. Also finely chop the liver, fry it and add it to the mixture. Now lightly fry the whole mixture together and fill the intestines, which have previously been cut into smaller sections. Tie them at the ends, prick them at intervals and boil them in salted water. Thereafter, fry the sausages until they brown. Remove them from the pan to a plate, and dust with sugar, cinnamon and sesame.

Pigs' intestines

1 pig's liver

1 ½ cups of raisins

1 ½ cups of walnuts or white almonds

½ kg coarse-milled wheat

Sesame

3 lemons

3 bitter oranges

½ cup oil

Salt, pepper, cinnamon

Pork in wine

Wash the meat well, and cut it into small pieces. Heat the oil to a high temperature in a pan. Carefully add the meat and fry it. When it is half done add the wine, salt and pepper, cover the pan and leave it to cook over a low heat until only the oil is left with the meat.

½ kg pork

½ cup red wine

Salt, pepper

½ cup olive oil

Pork with wheat grains

Wash the meat, cut it into small pieces and leave it to drain. Heat the oil to a high temperature in a pan and sauté the onion and meat. Pour over the lemon juice, add 1 cup of water, lower the heat and leave to simmer gently for about 1 hour.When the meat is almost cooked, add 3-4 cups of water and as soon as it comes to the boil add the wheat and seasoning. Leave to cook over a low heat for about another quarter of an hour.

1 kg pork

2 cups of wheat grains

3 tbs oil

1 large onion

1 lemon

Salt, pepper

Brawn made from a pig's head

1 medium-sized pig's head

2-3 hard-boiled eggs

4 carrots

Salt, pepper

Lemon juice

Wash the head, leave for a few hours and wash it again. Boil it in a large amount of water, initially removing the scum with a slotted spoon, and then add the carrots and seasonings. Cover the pan and leave the head to simmer for several hours. When it is ready, strain it and place it on a plate. Strain the liquid through a sieve and return it to the pan. Cut the carrots into little pieces and place them in moulds. Do the same with the eggs, arranging them in patterns on the base of the moulds so that the brawn will have a nice pattern on the surface when it is turned out of the mould. Meanwhile cut up the lean meat from the head into small pieces and put them to boil once again in the liquid. Turn off the heat and add the lemon juice. Finally, with a spoon, add the liquid and pieces of meat to the moulds containing the carrots and eggs, taking care not to dislodge them. Leave the liquid to cool and then transfer the moulds to the refrigerator. When the brawn has finally set, turn it out from the moulds to serve.

Sinklina (pork preserved in fat)

Lean pork meat
Aromatic herbs (sage, thyme, rosemary, oregano)

Cut the meat into strips, sprinkle with salt and hang them above the fire or in a fireplace, about 1 metre apart. Set alight to the aromatic herbs, cover them with ash to form thick smoke and leave the meat to smoke for several hours. When it has browned and cooked, wash it well, drain it and cut into small pieces. Place them in a clay pot and cover with pork fat to preserve them. Take out from the pot the exact amount of smoked pork that you need each time. It can be cooked as ordinary meat (along with potatoes, greens eggs etc) but the cooking time will be longer.

Browned pork

Wash the meat, cut it into pieces and season. Pour the oil into the pan and when it is hot add the meat, taking care that all the pieces touch the bottom of the pan. Turn the pieces frequently until they are browned. Reduce the heat, add the rosemary, cover the pan and leave the meat to cook in the oil and its own juices until it is tender.

1½ kg pork
½ cup oil
Rosemary
Salt

Tzoulamas from Heraklion

Cut the liver into small pieces, season, and fry it. Add about 1 litre of water and as soon as it boils, add the rice. A little before the rice is cooked, add the raisins and almonds and stir well together. Remove from the heat. Spread three sheets of fyllo pastry in an oiled dish. Dust the pastry with cinnamon and sugar, spread half of the filling over it and place another 3 sheets of fyllo pastry on top. Dust again with sugar and cinnamon and place the rest of the filling on top. Cover with more fyllo pastry and also dust in the same way, also adding the remainder of the oil and half a cup of water. Bake the tzoulamas for half an hour in a medium oven, until the top has browned.

½ kg pork liver
200 gr sugar
½ kg rice
200 gr raisins
200 gr almonds
½ cup oil or butter
½ tsp cinnamon
Salt, pepper
½ kg fyllo pastry

Youvarlakia
(boiled meat balls)

Put the minced beef, onion, rice, parsley and one cup of water into a bowl and mix well, finally adding the meringue. Form the mixture into little balls and roll them in flour. Bring 2 litres of water to the boil and then add a little salt, oil, and the meat balls. Leave to cook for about 1 ½ hours. When they are ready, beat the egg yolks and without stopping, add the lemon juice and a little of the liquid from the pan. Add this mixture to the pan and shake to distribute it evenly. Turn off the heat and serve immediately.

1 kg minced beef
1 coffee cup of rice
2 chopped onions
3 tbs flour
3 egg yolks
1 egg white beaten to a meringue
Juice of 2 lemons
1 bunch of finely chopped parsley
Salt, pepper
1 cup oil

Soutzoukakia (spicy meat rissoles)

Mix the meat in a bowl with the stale bread (which you have first soaked in the wine), the pounded garlic, egg, salt, pepper and cumin. When the ingredients are well mixed, form spherical or elongated soutzoukakia and leave them to rest for about an hour. Then heat the oil to a very high temperature in a pan and lightly fry the soutzoukakia. Add the chopped tomatoes, 1 cup of water, and a little salt, and as soon as the sauce begins to thicken transfer both soutzoukakia and sauce to a baking dish. Cook in the oven for around half an hour.

½ kg minced meat

2 slices of stale bread

4-5 ripe tomatoes

2 cloves of garlic

1 egg

½ cup red wine

½ tsp cumin

Salt, pepper

½ cup oil

Minced beef with macaroni

Heat the oil in a pan and add the minced meat. Stir for a few minutes, add the finely chopped onion and sauté all together. Pour over the wine and add the finely chopped tomatoes. Season, and if necessary add a little water. Cover the pan and leave the meat to cook over a moderate heat, until it is tender in the sauce.

Meanwhile, boil the macaroni in a large quantity of salted water. Drain, and if liked, 'singe' with a little oil (heat a little oil to a high temperature in a pan, turn off the heat and add the macaroni, stirring so that it is all coated with the oil). Serve the macaroni on a plate with the meat sauce poured over it.

½ kg minced beef

1 onion

2-3 ripe tomatoes

½ glass of red wine

½ kg macaroni
(use spaghetti)

½ cup oil

Salt, pepper

Meat rissoles with potatoes in the oven

Peel and wash the potatoes, then cut them into medium-sized pieces. Season with salt and spread them out in a baking dish. Make the rissoles: mix the meat in a large bowl with the bread, egg, finely chopped onion, salt and pepper. Form into medium-sized balls and place them on top of the potatoes. At the same time, make the sauce: heat the oil in a pan and sauté the finely chopped onion. Add the tomatoes, also finely chopped, salt, pepper, sugar, thyme and one cup of water. Allow the sauce to simmer for about 10 minutes. Pour over the meat rissoles and place the dish in the oven for about 1 hour.

1 kg minced meat (pork and beef mixed)

3 slices of bread, soaked in water and squeezed well

1 egg

1 onion

Salt, pepper

4-5 medium-sized potatoes

For the sauce:

3-4 ripe tomatoes

1 onion

1 tsp sugar

Salt, pepper, thyme

½ cup oil

Aubergine 'little shoes'

½ kg beef mince

11 elongated aubergines

2 finely chopped onions

1 bunch finely chopped parsley

3 finely chopped tomatoes

Cinnamon

Salt, pepper

1 cup oil

Wash the aubergines, cut away a long slice along their length and scoop out the flesh with a spoon, so that they resemble 'boats'. The stem can be left on. Fry them lightly and allow them to drain until you proceed to prepare the meat. Put ½ cup of oil into a pan, bring it to a high heat and sauté the onions. Add the meat and stir together. Add the tomatoes, parsely, cinnamon, salt and pepper and allow to cook for about half and hour. Put the aubergines into a baking dish, fill them with the meat mixture and if liked, add a layer of béchamel on top. Bake for about 30 miniutes.

Cabbage 'dolmades' with egg and lemon

Set a saucepan of water to boil. Meanwhile, remove the outer leaves from the cabbage (retain them for later use) and cut into the base of the stalk deeply and in a circular motion, until you reach the centre of the cabbage. Place it in the water with the base of the stalk downwards and leave it to cook until it softens. Remove from the heat, drain it well and when it is cold, separate off the leaves. If the cabbage is large, cut it into two, removing the thick parts.

For the filling: finely chop the onion and sauté it in the oil. Add the meat, seasonings, oregano and a little water and allow all to boil once or twice. Now add the rice, stir the mixture well and allow it to come to the boil again. When the filling is ready, spread the outer leaves of the cabbage which you have retained over the base of a pan. Now place 1 tbs of the filling on each leaf, roll it up, and arrange the rolls on the cabbage leaves in the pan. If there are a lot of rolls, arrange them in two layers. Spread leaves over the second layer again. Add one glass of water and cover the dolmades with a plate, so that they remain immobile and do not come apart. Place the pan on a medium heat and cook for about ¾ hour.

Make the sauce as follows: melt the butter, add the flour and stir well together until

1 white cabbage
½ kg pork mince
1 cup rice for filling
1 onion
2-3 cloves of garlic
1 cup oil
Salt, pepper, oregano

Sauce:
2 eggs
Juice of 2 lemons
2 tbs butter
2 tbs flour

slightly browned. Remove the pan from the heat and add a little of the juices from the dolmades, stirring constantly to avoid lumps. Beat the eggs and gradually add the lemon. Mix the butter mixture with the lemon and return the sauce to a low heat, taking care that it does not boil. When the dolmades are ready, remove the large cabbage leaves from the top of the pan, and serve the dolmades on a plate with the sauce poured over them.

Moussaka

Cut the vegetables into slices and fry each type separately. Heat the oil and sauté the onion with the meat. Add the chopped tomatoes, parsley, salt and pepper and leave to simmer for about 20 minutes. Spread a layer of fried potatoes in a dish, put a layer of courgettes on top, and then the meat mixture and the aubergines. Finally, pour over a layer of béchamel and put the dish into a preheated oven for about 45 minutes.

700 gr minced beef
2 large aubergines
1 kg potatoes
4-5 courgettes
2 tomatoes
1 onion
Parsley
Salt, pepper
1/2 cup oil and extra oil for frying
Béchamel (see 'sauces')

Keftedakia

Mix together all the ingredients (apart from the flour) in a bowl to a homogeneous mass. Form into balls, roll them in flour and fry in very hot oil, turning them constantly so that they do not burn and are cooked from all sides.

½ kg minced meat

4 slices of bread, soaked in water, or 100 gr breadcrumbs

1 finely chopped onion

1 egg

3 tbs oil

Vinegar

Salt, pepper, oregano

1 cup flour

Oil for frying

Stuffed courgettes with egg and lemon

Wash the courgettes, remove a little from the top and bottom and then remove the flesh with a teaspoon or a corer (retain 1 cup of the flesh for use in the recipe). Salt the inside surfaces, cover them, and then prepare the filling: Heat a little oil to a high temperature and sauté the meat with the onion. Turn off the heat and add the rice, finely chopped parsley, 1 cup of the flesh from the courgettes, salt and pepper. Stir well together and fill the courgettes with the mixture. Do not overfill, as the rice will swell. Place them in a pan either slightly tilted on their sides or standing upright, and add the oil, 2 cups of water, salt and pepper. Cover the pan, turn the heat to low, and cook for about 1 ½ hours, adding more water if necessary, so that a good amount of sauce is formed. When the food is ready, prepare the egg and lemon as follows: beat the eggs and without stopping, add the lemon juice and a little of the sauce from the pan. Pour it over the courgettes, shaking the pan to distribute it evenly, and turn off the heat.

1.5 kg courgettes
½ kg minced beef
½ kg long-grain rice
1 onion
½ bunch parsley
1 cup oil
Salt, pepper

Egg and lemon sauce
2 egg yolks
2 lemons

Snails

Place the snails in a bowl with water to soften and then with a little knife remove the impurities from the shells. Wash them well and leave to drain. Heat the oil to a high temperature and sauté the onions and garlic. Add the chopped tomatoes, vinegar, rosemary, salt and pepper and 1 cup of water. Allow to simmer for about 10 minutes and then add the snails. Cook for a further half an hour.

1 kg large snails
4-5 tomatoes
½ kg onions
½ whole garlic
½ cup vinegar
1 sprig of rosemary
Salt, pepper
1 ½ cups olive oil

Snails in the frying pan ('bourbouristi')

Place the snails in a bowl with water to soften and then with a little knife remove the impurities from their shells. Place a frying pan on the heat and cover the base of it with salt. Scatter the snails over the salt with the shells upwards and leave for a while. Now add the oil and a few minutes later, the vinegar and rosemary. Cover the pan and when the contents come to the boil, reduce the heat.

½ kg snails
1 cup vinegar
1 sprig of rosemary
Salt
½ cup oil

Snails with wheat grains

Wash the snails and boil them for a short time in salted water, so that they soften. After you have cleaned them, put the oil in a pan and sauté the snails together with the finely chopped onion. Now add the finely chopped tomatoes, salt, pepper and 2 cups of water. Lower the heat and leave the snails to cook. When ready, remove them from the pan with a slotted spoon and set aside. Add the wheat grains to the sauce, add 6 cups of water (ratio of wheat/water = 1/3) and allow it to cook over a low heat, stirring occasionally to prevent sticking. When the wheat has absorbed the water and swollen (after about 15 minutes) turn off the heat and add the snails to the pan. Mix well together and the food is ready to serve.

½ kg snails
2 cups wheat grains
½ cup oil
5 tomatoes
1 onion
Salt, pepper

ΦΕΤΑ-ΨΗΤΑ
€ 5,

ΣΑΡΔΕΛΑ
€ 5,

SEAFOOD & FISH

Β. Σ. ΚΙΟΥΡΤΖ

Cuttlefish in wine sauce

Remove the hard parts and the ink from the cuttlefish and cut them into medium-sized pieces. Pour the oil into a pan and sauté the onions, finely chopped, with the cuttlefish. As soon as they brown, pour over the wine and add the finely chopped tomatoes and tomato paste. Season and add the bay leaf. Stir well, lower the heat, cover the pan and leave to cook until the cuttlefish are tender and left only with their sauce.

1 kg cuttlefish

3 medium-sized onions

1 cup white wine

1 cup oil

3 ripe tomatoes

1 cup tomato paste

1 bay leaf

Salt, pepper

Cuttlefish with fennel

Wash, prepare and boil the cuttlefish. When they are tender, remove them from the pan and cut into pieces. Cut up and boil the fennel. Place together in a pan the oil, fennel, finely chopped onions, cuttlefish, salt and pepper. Cook for about half and hour and when ready, add the lemon juice into which you have beaten the flour; this will bind the sauce.

1 kg cuttlefish
1 kg fennel
2 spring onions
1 tbs flour
1 lemon
Salt, pepper
1 cup olive oil

Cuttlefish with spinach

Remove the hard parts and the ink from the cuttlefish (if liked, retain a little ink and put it into a bowl of water) and cut them into pieces. Pour the oil into a pan and sauté the finely chopped onion, fennel, dill, mint and finally, the cuttlefish. Pour over the wine and add a little of the water into which you put the ink, taking care not to stir up the water because this will cause the sand to swirl up and mix with it. Reduce the heat and leave the cuttlefish to cook until tender. Meanwhile, wash and finely chop the spinach. When the cuttlefish are partly cooked, add the spinach to the pan, season, mix well and allow it to cook with the cuttlefish over a low heat for about another 15-20 minutes.

1 kg cuttlefish

1½ kg spinach

1 cup oil

3 onions

1 bunch of fennel

1 bunch of dill

A few mint leaves

1 cup white wine

Salt, pepper

Cuttlefish with their ink

Remove the hard parts and the ink from the cuttlefish. Retain the ink from about 3-4 cuttlefish and place it in a bowl with water, so that the sand in the ink sinks to the bottom. Wash the cuttlefish and cut into pieces. Heat the oil to a high temperature in a pan and sauté the finely chopped onions and cuttlefish pieces until they are lightly browned. Pour over the wine, add 1 cup of water with the ink from the bowl, and then another cup of water. Stir well, cover the pan, lower the heat and cook for about half and hour, until the cuttlefish are tender and left with only a thickish sauce.

1 kg cuttlefish
1 cup oil
2 onions
½ cup white wine
Salt, pepper

Stuffed cuttlefish

Prepare the cuttlefish, removing the hard parts and the ink. Wash them and leave to drain. Prepare, wash and chop the spinach into large pieces. Sauté for 5 minutes in half of the oil with 1 finely chopped onion. Now stuff the cuttlefish with the spinach. Close them carefully and place them in a pan with the remaining oil and chopped onions. Sauté for a few minutes and then 'quench' with the wine. A few minutes later, add the chopped tomatoes, finely chopped fennel, seasonings and a little water. Leave to cook over a low heat until the cuttlefish are tender.

1 kg cuttlefish

1½ kg spinach

1 bunch of fennel

3 onions

1 cup oil

3 ripe tomatoes

1 cup red wine

Salt, pepper

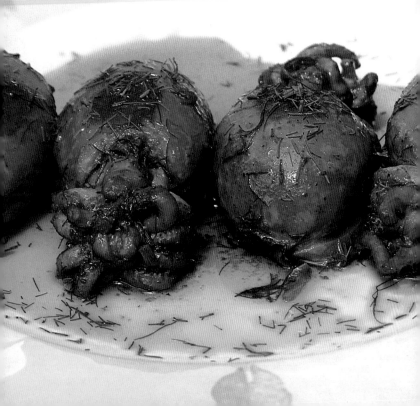

Lemon cod

Place the cod in a good amount of water to remove the salt and leave overnight. Next day, heat the oil to a high temperature in a pan and add the finely chopped onion and spring onions, allowing them to stew. Add 2 cups of water and as soon as it boils add the dill and parsley. Meanwhile, prepare, wash and cut the cod into portions and put them into the pan with the seasonings; allow to cook for about 20 minutes. Mix the flour with a little water, the lemon juice and a little of the liquid from the pan and pour it over the fish. Bring it to the boil once again.

½ kg dried, salted cod

1 onion

1 bunch spring onions

Dill

Parsley

2 tbs flour

1 lemon

Pepper

½ cup olive oil

Fried salted, dried cod

Place the cod in a good amount of water to remove the salt and leave overnight. Next day, wash it well, prepare it and cut into portions. Beat together the flour, salt, beaten egg and a little water to make a batter, dip the cod pieces in it and then fry them in very hot olive oil.

This dish goes very well with skordalia (see sauces).

½ kg salted, dried cod

1 egg

1 cup flour

Olive oil for frying

Salted, dried cod with 'barbouni' beans

Cut the salted, dried cod into pieces and place it in a bowl of water overnight to remove the salt. Next day, heat the oil in a pan and sauté the finely chopped onion and the cod until it is lightly browned. Add a little water and leave to cook over a low heat for about 10 minutes. Meanwhile, bring the beans to the boil once or twice in enough plain water to cover. Drain them, and add them to the pan containing the cod. Add the finely chopped tomatoes, salt, pepper and water to cover. Remove the cod from the pan and leave the beans to cook for about half an hour. When they are partly cooked, return the cod to the pan and allow everything to cook for about another half hour.

1 kg salted, dried cod

½ kg 'barbouni' beans

1 onion

3 tomatoes

1 cup oil

Salt, pepper

Stuffed squid

Remove the hard parts, ink and eyes of the squid. Pull off the tentacles and chop them. Wash the squid well, removing the dark membrane and leaving only the white flesh. Put half of the oil into a pan and sauté the finely chopped onions. Add the tentacles, stir well together and add the finely chopped dill, seasonings and 1 cup of water. Lower the heat and after about a quarter of an hour add the rice and two cups of water. As soon as the rice is cooked, turn off the heat, add the lemon juice and leave the mixture to cool. Fill the squid using a teaspoon, taking care to leave a space for the rice to swell. Close the squid with toothpicks and place them in a baking dish, close to each other. Pour over the remaining oil and ½ cup of water, season well, cover the dish

1 kg medium-sized squid
1 cup oil
1 cup rice
2 onions
1 bunch of dill
Salt, pepper
1 lemon

Fried squid

Prepare and wash the squid. Mix the flour with the salt, roll the squid in the mixture and fry them in very hot oil, turning constantly. When they are ready, remove them from the pan with a slotted spoon and place them on kitchen paper on a plate, to drain. Serve hot garnished with lemon slices.

1 kg squid

Flour

2 lemons

Salt

Olive oil for frying

for the first part of the cooking time with aluminium foil, and bake in the oven for about half and hour.

If liked, the squid can also be cooked on the top of the stove in a pan; in that case, add the oil, enough water to cover, the juice of another lemon and season well. Cover the pan and leave to cook until the squid are tender and most of the liquid has been absorbed. To serve, the small amount of sauce that remains can be bound with a little corn flour and poured over the squid.

Squid in a red sauce

Wash the squid and cut into pieces. Heat the oil to a very high temperature and sauté the finely chopped onion and garlic. Add the squid, finely chopped tomatoes and parsley, salt, pepper, oregano and a little water. Cover the pan, lower the heat and leave to cook for about 1 hour, until the squid are tender and left with a thickish sauce.

1 kg large squid

1 cup oil

1 onion

1 clove of garlic

2 tomatoes

1 bunch of parsley

Salt, pepper, oregano

Octopus with short macaroni shells

Place the octopus in water the night before you intend to cook it, for it to tenderize. If it is already soft, cut it into pieces, wash them and leave to strain. Heat the oil in a pan and sauté the finely chopped onion. Add the octopus, stir well and 'quench' with the wine. Add water and leave to cook over a low heat. When it is partly cooked, add the finely chopped tomatoes, salt, and pepper and leave to cook well. Remove the octopus from the pan with a slotted spoon and cook the macaroni in the sauce that has remained, adding water if necessary. Mix together the octopus and the macaroni and serve hot.

1 kg octopus
½ kg short macaroni shells
3-4 ripe tomatoes
1 large onion
½ cup red wine
Salt, pepper
1 cup olive oil

Octopus in wine

Wash the octopus well. Remove the beak, eyes, and the ink from the stomach sac. Cut the octopus into small pieces and place in a pan over a low heat for about half an hour, without water, to cook in their own moisture; cover the pan. When the octopus is soft, strain off the water and retain it for later use; add the oil and finely chopped onion. As soon as the contents of the pan come to the boil, 'quench' them with the wine and then add the chopped tomatoes and bay leaves. Cover the pan and leave to cook over a low heat until the octopus is really tender and the sauce has thickened. If necessary, add a little of the retained liquid or some more wine. Do not add water, otherwise the octopus will toughen.

1 kg octopus

1 small onion

1/2 cup oil

1 cup wine

3-4 tomatoes

1-2 bay leaves

Pepper

Octopus in vinegar

Wash the octopus and boil it in enough water to cover with the finely chopped onions. When it is tender, remove it from the heat and cut into small pieces. Place them in a bowl and add the oil, vinegar, oregano, salt and pepper. Keep covered in the refrigerator and serve cold as an appetizer.

2 kg octopus
2 onions
½ cup oil
Vinegar
Oregano
Salt, pepper

Octopus with potatoes

1 kg octopus

1 kg potatoes

4 tomatoes

3 onions

3 cloves of garlic

1 cup oil

1 bay leaf

Salt, pepper

Wash the octopus and boil it in enough water to cover, until it has softened. Strain and cut the octopus into pieces; retain the cooking liquid for later use. Finely chop the onion and sauté it in very hot oil. Add the chopped tomatoes, finely chopped garlic, bay leaf, potatoes cut into large pieces, octopus, and the liquid. If needed, add a little more water. Season well and cook until a thick sauce is left.

Boiled fish and fish soup

Prepare and wash the fish and the vegetables. Cut the carrots, celery, potatoes and onion into medium-sized pieces and leave the courgettes whole. Half-fill a saucepan with water and add the oil, carrots, onions and celery. Boil for about 15 minutes and then add the potatoes, courgettes, fish and seasonings. After about half an hour, when the fish and vegetables have cooked,

2 kg fish (grouper, bass, cod, rascasse etc)

1/2 kg courgettes

1/2 kg carrots

3 potatoes

2 onions

1/2 cup oil

1 bunch of celery

1/2 cup rice

Salt, pepper

2 egg yolks

2 lemons

remove them from the pan with a slotted spoon and transfer to a plate. If liked, retain about half of the vegetables and one piece of the fish, pulp them through a sieve and add them to the liquid in the pan. Bring to the boil and add the rice. Leave to cook for 20 minutes until soft and then turn off the heat. Make the egg and lemon mixture: Beat the yolks of the eggs and without stopping gradually add the lemon juice and a little of the soup. Now pour the mixture into the pan, stir well, and the soup is ready.

Anchovies with oregano

1 kg anchovies

2 lemons

1 tsp oregano

Salt, pepper

½ cup olive oil

Prepare and clean the anchovies, discarding the heads. Rinse well. Place them in a dish, dust with oregano, sprinkle over the lemon juice, season and add a little water, and bake in the oven for about 40 minutes.

Fish in the oven

Clean and prepare the fish, wash it and if large, cut it into slices. Season, sprinkle over the lemon juice and leave to one side. Prepare the sauce: Heat the oil in a pan and sauté the finely chopped onions and garlic. Add the finely chopped parsley, organo, and 'quench' with the wine. Add the chopped tomatoes and seasoning, then bring to the boil once or twice to thicken. Spread the fish out in a baking dish and pour over the sauce. Place in the oven and leave to cook at a moderate temperature for about one hour.

1 kg large fish

1 cup oil

2 onions

2 cloves of garlic

½ bunch of parsley

1 glass of white wine

3 tomatoes

Juice of 1 lemon

Salt, pepper, oregano

Little cheese envelopes with honey

Beat the eggs and add the oil. Mix well together and add 1 cup of water, the baking soda and the flour, to form a moderately stiff dough. Leave aside, wrapped in a teacloth, and prepare the filling: mix together the cheese and eggs, cinnamon and mint. Now roll out the dough into a sheet, using a rolling pin (or a pasta machine). Cut out circles with a glass. Place a teaspoon of the filling on each circle and fold it over to form a closed half-moon shape. Heat some oil to a high temperature and fry the envelopes. Serve hot, with honey.

For the pastry:

1 kg flour

2 eggs

½ tsp baking soda

1/3 cup oil

Filling:

1 kg myzithra (cream cheese)

2 eggs

1 tsp cinnamon

A little chopped mint

Honey

Lychnarakia ('little lights')

Prepare the pastry dough by mixing the ingredients together and then set it aside, covered with a cloth. In a bowl, mix the myzithra and the crumbled anthotyro well together with the eggs and mint. Roll out the dough into a sheet. Using a cup or a glass (according to the desired size of the lychnarakia) cut out rounds and place a teaspoon of the cheese filling on each. Close them, forming half-moon shapes. The pastry sheet can also be cut into square pieces, the filling placed on top and then the four sides folded over towards the centre leaving a little of the filling visible. Whatever shape is chosen, place the lychnarakia on an oiled baking sheet and brush them with egg. A little sesame may also be scattered over them. Bake for about an hour in a moderate oven.

Pastry:

½ kg flour

1 cup milk

1 tbs olive oil

As much water as needed

Filling:

½ kg myzithra (cream cheese)

½ kg anthotyro (soft cheese)

4 eggs

1-2 mint leaves

Xerotigana

Mix together the oil, sugar and raki in a bowl and slowly add the flour and water. When the dough is formed (it must be quite firm) leave it to rest for about 1 hour. Then, either in the traditional way by hand or using a machine, roll it into a thin sheet and then cut it into strips 3 cms wide and 30-40 cms long. Heat the oil well in a frying pan and then take each strip separately, spear one end on a fork and place it in the very hot oil, winding the strip around the fork in the pan to form a nest. Alternately, roll them up before they are put into the hot oil. As soon as they brown, they are ready. Remove from the heat and drain on kitchen paper to remove the excess oil. Prepare a light syrup by boiling the sugar with the water. When the xerotigana have cooled, dip them individually into the syrup for a minute or two. Transfer them to a plate and scatter the walnuts, sesame and cinnamon over them.

They can be prepared without syrup; simply pour honey over them and scatter over the walnuts, sesame and cinnamon.

1 kg coarse flour
1/2 cup sugar
1 little glass of raki
1 cup of chopped walnuts
1/2 cup sesame
Cinnamon
Honey
1 cup olive oil
Oil for frying

Syrup:
1 1/2 cups sugar
2 1/2 cups water

Sfakian pies

Put the flour in a bowl and add the salt. Open a well in the centre and pour in the oil, raki and water. Mix to a moderate to soft dough. Mash the cheese with a fork. Divide the dough into ten little balls and roll them out; place 1 tbs of myzithra on top of each. Draw in the edges of the pastry towards the centre to cover the filling, forming a ball. Roll each out again, this time into a round about the size of a fruit plate. Fry them one by one in a very hot pan with very little oil, turning them constantly so that they do not burn. Pour over honey to serve.

Pastry:
½ kg flour
1 tsp salt
2 tbs oil
3 tbs raki
1 cup of water

Filling:
½ kg myzithra (cream cheese)
cinnamon

Honey to serve

Sarikopites

Put the flour in a bowl and open up a well in the centre. Add the oil, raki and salt. Mix to a dough, adding the water gradually, as much as is required, to form a moderate to firm dough. When it is ready form it into a ball, cover and leave to rest for one hour. Meanwhile, put the cheese into a bowl and mash it with a fork. Roll out the dough into a thin sheet and cut into long strips about 20 x 7 cms. Spread a spoonful of cheese along the whole length, roll it up in the same direction and close the edges well. Now bend the strips into a snail shape to form the sarikopites. Fry them in very hot oil and serve either dusted with cinnamon and sugar or with honey.

Pastry:
½ kg flour
3 tbs oil
2 tbs raki
Salt
1 cup of water

½ kg xinomyzithra (cream cheese)
Honey (or sugar and cinnamon)
Oil for frying

Loukoumades
(honey puffs) with yeast

Put the yeast into 1 cup of the warm water and stir it well to dissolve it. Put the flour, salt, yeast, honey and the remainder of the water into a bowl and mix well to a batter with a spoon. Cover the mixture and leave in a warm place to rise. When the mixture has almost doubled and there are bubbles on the surface, it is ready. Pour a good amount of olive oil into a pan and bring it to a very high temperature. With your hand, take a small amount of the mixture, clench your fist and with a spoon remove the mixture that oozes out. Toss the content of your hand into the oil and repeat until the pan is full. Allow the loukoumades to brown, remove them with a slotted spoon and place them to drain on absorbent paper. Serve hot, with honey and sesame.

½ kg flour
1 tbs salt
1 level tbs honey
2 ½ cups of water
½ envelope yeast
Oil for frying

To serve:
Honey
Sesame

Mamoulia, from Rethymnon

Put the butter into a saucepan and as soon as it has melted, add the sugar which has previously been dissolved in milk. Stirring continuously, add the flour until a firm dough is formed. Remove from the heat and when the mixture has cooled, add the beaten eggs and the baking soda dissolved in the raki. Mix to a dough again, until a soft and pliable mass is achieved. Prepare the filling as follows: Mix together the walnuts, almonds, sugar and cinnamon. Now cut off a piece of dough and flatten it out over the palm of your hand. Put a little spoonful of the filling on it and close it well. Put the 'mamoulia' on a buttered baking sheet and bake in a moderate oven for about half and hour. Immediately on removing them from the oven, sprinkle over the flower water and powdered sugar.

350 gr butter
½ cup sugar
½ cup milk
5 cups flour
2 eggs
1 little glass of raki
½ tsp baking soda

Filling:
½ kg walnuts and almonds, chopped
4-5 tbs sugar
1 tsp cinnamon

Flower water
Powdered sugar

Koutalites ('spoon' fritters)

Mix the flour with the salt, water and honey to form a moderately thick batter. Heat the oil in a pan. Using a spoon (Greek 'koutali', hence their name) drop amounts of the mixture into the very hot oil. Be sure to have a bowl of water to hand, in which to plunge the spoon before dipping it into the mixture, so that it does not stick. Fry the fritters on both sides so that they brown. Drain on a plate, on absorbent paper, and serve hot, either with honey and sesame or sugar and cinnamon.

½ kg flour
1 tbs salt
1 level tbs honey
2 ½ cups of water
Oil for frying

To decorate:
Honey and sesame, or sugar and cinnamon

Kataïfi

In a large bowl mix the walnuts, almonds, toast crumbs, sugar, cinnamon powder and clove to form the filling. Put the oil into a little bowl, dip your fingers into it and pull out the pastry strands. By this means, the pastry receives as much oil as it needs, evenly distributed. Now take a little of it, put a spoonful of the filling on it, and roll it up to form a sausage. Repeat until all the filling and pastry has been used, and then place the rolls in a dish close to each other. When the dish is full, sprinkle over a little water. Bake in a moderate oven for about half and hour until the rolls begin to brown. Care is needed, as the pastry burns easily. Remove the dish from the oven, prepare the syrup by mixing all the ingredients in a saucepan and bringing them to the boil a few time until the syrup thickens. When it is ready and still hot, pour it over the rolls, cover them and allow them to cool.

1 kg kataïfi pastry
1/2 kg chopped walnuts
1/2 kg chopped almonds
3 pieces of toast, crumbed
1/2 cup sugar
Cinnamon powder
Ground clove
1 cup oil

Syrup:
6 cups of water
6 cups sugar
2 tbs honey
1 cinnamon stick

Galatopita

Butter each sheet of fyllo on both sides. Crumple them up and place them side by side in a baking dish. Beat the sugar with the eggs and stir in the milk. Pour the mixture over the crumpled sheets of fyllo and bake in a moderate oven until the top has browned.

3 cups of milk
1 cup sugar
3 eggs
8 sheets of fyllo pastry
A little butter

Tzevremedakia

Begin by making the syrup, since this must be quite cold when we remove the tzevremedakia from the oven. Put the water, sugar and orange slices into a pan and boil them until a syrup is formed. This should be quite thin - certainly thinner than the syrup used in 'spoon sweets'.

Remove the syrup from the heat and leave to cool completely.

Make the filling by mashing the myzithra and mixing it with the egg and cinnamon (optional). Fold the fyllo pastry in half and cut it into two. Fold it in half again and cut it, thus forming pieces measuring about 20 x 22 cms.

For each tzevremedaki, take two of the sheets of fyllo, oil them and place them on top of each other.

Along the length of the bottom spread a spoonful of the filling and in order to retain it fold over the two sides. Brush the inside of the tzevremedaki with oil and roll up the filling to form a cylinder. Place the rolls in a lightly oiled dish, not too close together, and brush their surfaces with oil. Preheat the oven to 180 C. Put in the dish and lower the heat to 160 C. After half and hour, raise the heat again to 180 C, in order to brown the pastry. As soon as the tzevremedakia are ready, remove them from the oven and pour over the cold syrup.

1 small whole myzithra

1 egg

1/2 tsp cinnamon (optional)

1/2 kg fyllo pastry

Syrup:

4 cups sugar

4 cups of water

1 orange cut into slices

Cake made with olive oil

Put the oil into a bowl with the sugar and beat very well together. Gradually add the eggs, milk, vanilla, and lemon zest and juice. Stir all well together then slowly add the flour, into which you have mixed the baking powder.

Oil the bottom of a cake tin and pour in the mixture. Bake the cake in a preheated oven for about 45 minutes. If liked, when the cake is removed from the tin it can be dusted with powdered sugar.

4 ½ cups flour

1 cup sugar

1½ cups milk

2 eggs

1 tsp baking powder

Juice and zest of 1 lemon

1 envelope vanilla

1½ cups oil

Poura (walnut rolls)

Prepare the syrup, so that it will be cold when the poura are cooked: boil the water with the sugar and orange slices until a syrup is formed, but not as thick as that for poura.

Mix together the chopped walnuts, sugar, breadcrumbs, cinnamon and sesame.

Cut the fyllo pastry exactly as for tzevremedakia, take two of them, brush with oil on the inside and spread the filling over the whole surface (i.e. not as in tzevremedakia, where it is only spread along one side).

Fold over the sides so that the filling cannot escape, brush the inside with oil and roll up into a cylinder. Arrange in a lightly oiled dish, not too close together, and brush the surfaces with oil.

Bake in a preheated oven, exactly as for tzevremedakia. As soon as they are ready, remove from the oven and pour over the cold syrup.

½ kg fyllo pastry
½ kg chopped walnuts
2 tbs sugar
2 tbs breadcrumbs
1 tsp cinnamon
4 tbs sesame

Syrup:
4 cups sugar
4 cups of water
1 orange cut into slices

Galaktoboureko

Butter a baking dish and spread out half of the fyllo pastry in it, buttering each sheet as you lay it on top of the other. Butter the remaining sheets in the same way and set them aside. If using fresh milk, boil it and then allow it to cool. Beat the eggs in your mixer with the extra yolks and sugar. Transfer the mixture to a saucepan and gradually add the milk and semolina. Simmer gently until the mixture thickens. Remove from the heat and add any remaining butter. Pour the filling into the dish, over the fyllo pastry, and cover with the remaining buttered sheets. Score the pastry, so that the galatoboureko will cut easily into portions when cooked. Bake in the oven at 190 C for about 15 minutes and then reduce to 160 C and bake for a further 35 minutes. Meanwhile, make the syrup by boiling the water, sugar and lemon zest together. When you remove the galatoboureko from the oven, immediately pour the syrup (which should have cooled) over it.

300 gr fyllo pastry
½ cup butter
4 cups milk
½ cup sugar
2 eggs + 2 yolks
5 tbs fine semolina
Vanilla

Syrup:
2 cups sugar
1 cup water
Lemon zest

Cake with apples

Beat together the sugar with the oil (or margarine) in your mixer. Add the egg yolks, and then the whites beaten separately to a stiff meringue. Sprinkle the apples with cognac, scatter 2 tbs of sugar over them and add them to the egg mixture with the walnuts.

Finally, mix together the baking powder with the flour and add it slowly. Pour the mixture into an oiled cake tin and bake in a moderate oven for about 1 hour.

1/2 cup oil or 150 gr margarine

1 1/2 cups sugar

2 1/2 cups flour

4 eggs

1/2 envelope of baking powder

2 1/2 cups of finely chopped apples

1 cup walnuts

A little cognac

Almond cake

Beat the sugar with the egg yolks until the mixture whitens. Dissolve the baking powder in the cognac and add to the mixture along with the almonds, crumbed rusks, and lemon zest. Beat the egg whites to a stiff meringue and add to the mixture along with the salt. Pour the mixture into a buttered cake tin and bake in a moderate oven for about 45 minutes. Meanwhile, prepare the syrup and pour it over the cake as soon as it is removed from the oven.

3 cups chopped almonds

8 eggs

1 ½ cups sugar

3 rusks, crumbed

2 tsp baking powder

½ small wineglass of cognac

Zest of a lemon

1 pinch of salt

Syrup:

2 cups sugar

1 ½ cups of water

Juice of half a lemon

Almond macaroons

Beat the egg whites well. Add the sugar and continue beating until it is incorporated. Add the finely ground almonds and the lemon zest. Stir well together and form the macaroons like biscuits, placing them on an oiled baking sheet. Bake in a moderate oven for about 20 minutes, until they are browned.

1200 gr ground almonds

600 gr sugar

10 egg whites

Lemon zest

Walnut cake

Beat the oil and the sugar well together, in your mixer. Add the eggs, milk, walnuts, cinnamon, cloves and finally the flour into which you have mixed the baking powder. Pour into an oiled cake tin and bake in a moderate oven for about 45 minutes. When the cake is cooked, allow it to cool and then remove from the tin. Prepare the syrup: Boil the water in a saucepan, add the sugar and then the cognac. Stir well together and leave to boil for about 5 minutes, to form a light syrup. Pour the syrup over the cake while it is still hot.

1 cup olive oil

1 1/2 cups sugar

6 eggs

1 cup milk

1 tbs cinnamon

3-4 ground cloves

3 cups chopped walnuts

1/2 kg flour

2 tsp baking powder

Syrup:

2 cups sugar

2 cups of water

2 tsp cognac

Vasilopita

Cream together the sugar and butter in your mixer. Without stopping the machine, add the egg yolks, milk, almonds (roughly chopped) and the cognac.

Dissolve the baking soda in the lemon juice and add to the mixture along with the vanilla. Add the flour mixed with the baking powder.

Finally, beat the egg whites in a separate bowl to a stiff meringue and add to the mixture, lightly incorporating them with a spoon, so that the meringue does not 'deflate'. Pour the mixture into a buttered tin and bake in a moderate oven for about 1 hour.

1 cup sugar
1 cup butter
7 eggs
1 cup milk
150 gr almonds
1/2 cup cognac
1 tsp baking soda
Juice of 1/2 lemon
1 tsp vanilla
1 tsp baking powder
3 cups flour

Ravani

Boil and mince the rice. Put 2 litres of water into a pan with the sugar and leave it to boil. Now add half of the oil, the rice and the almonds. Beat well until you achieve a dense, smooth paste. When it is ready, spread the mixture in a buttered tin and dust with cinnamon. Score into sections, stick a clove in each, and bake in the oven for about an hour.

800 gr rice
1 kg sugar
1 cup chopped almonds
Cinnamon
Cloves
1 cup oil

Ravani with coconut

Beat the sugar and oil well together in the mixer and add the eggs one by one; then add the milk and the coconut. Finally, mix together the baking powder with the flour and add it gradually to the mixture, continuing to beat for a while.

Put the mixture into an oiled and lightly floured baking dish or mould and bake in a moderate oven for about one hour. In the meantime, prepare the syrup by boiling the water with the sugar and lemon peel for about five minutes.

When the ravani is ready, remove it from the tin and pour over the syrup.

2/3 cup oil
1 cup sugar
3 eggs
2/3 cups milk
1 1/2 cups coconut
1 1/2 cups flour
1 tsp baking powder

For the syrup:
1 1/2 cups sugar
1 1/2 cups of water
1 tsp lemon juice
Lemon peel

Apple cake

Beat the oil and 1 cup of sugar well together, using your mixer. Add the eggs and then, slowly, the flour mixed with the baking powder. The texture will be quite thick and almost crumbly.

Puree the apples and mix them with the remaining cup of sugar, cinnamon and walnuts. Take half of the cake mixture and rubbing it through your fingers, spread it over the bottom of a baking dish.

Pour the apple filling on top and then add the rest of the cake mixture in the same way. Bake in a moderate oven for about 30-40 minutes. Dust with powdered sugar when cold.

5 cups flour

2 cups sugar

2 eggs

2 tsp baking powder

1 cup chopped almonds

Cinnamon

6-7 apples

Powdered sugar

1 cup oil

Little apple pies

For the dough: Beat the oil and sugar well together in your mixer. Add the eggs, cognac, lemon zest and finally the flour mixed with the baking powder. For the filling: Wash, peel and grate the apples on a cheese grater and add them to the other ingredients.

Divide the dough into little balls and roll them out into little sheets. Put a teaspoon of the apple mixture on each. Fold over the dough to cover the filling and close them tightly to form semicircular envelopes. Place the apple pies on an oiled baking sheet and bake in a moderate oven for about 20 minutes. When they are lightly browned, remove from the oven, allow to cool, and served dusted with powdered sugar.

Dough:
3/4 cup oil
1/2 cup powdered sugar
1/2 kg flour
2 tsp baking powder
2 eggs
Zest of 1 lemon
1 small glass of cognac or raki

Filling:
1 kg apples
5 tbs sugar
1 tsp ground cinnamon
1 tsp ground cloves

Powdered sugar

Tahini cake

Beat the sugar and the tahini together in the mixer and then add the water and the remaining ingredients, keeping the walnuts until last.

Pour the mixture into a buttered dish and bake in a moderate oven.

Sprinkle over the powdered sugar and cinnamon.

1 1/2 cups tahini (sesame paste)
1 1/2 cups of water
1 cup sugar
1 cup raisins
1/2 kg flour
1 1/2 tbs baking soda
1 level tbs cinnamon
2 tsp ground cloves
1 1/2 cups walnuts
Powdered sugar

Raisin cake

Beat the oil and the sugar well together in a bowl. Dissolve the ammonia and baking soda in the orange juice and add to the oil and sugar mixture. Add the cinnamon, cloves, lemon zest and raisins. Slowly add the flour, and the mixture is ready.

Pour into an oiled baking tin and bake in a preheated oven for about 1 hour.

1 kg fine flour

½ kg sugar

1 glass of orange juice

1 tsp ground cinnamon

1 tsp baking soda

1 tsp ammonia

Zest of 1 lemon

1 cup of ground raisins

Ground cloves

2 cups oil

'Stafidota' (raisin pastries)

Beat the oil and sugar well together and add the orange juice, lemon zest, lye, cognac, cinnamon and cloves. Continue beating for about half an hour. Beat the baking soda with the lemon juice, add to the mixture and then slowly begin to add the flour.

When the dough is thick enough, roll it out into a sheet. Cut out rounds, using a glass. Place 1 tsp of the ground raisins on each and close over well to form a half-moon. Oil a baking sheet, place the pastries on it, and bake in a preheated oven.

1 kg flour
1½ cups flour
½ cup orange juice
Juice and zest of a lemon
½ cup lye
1 tsp baking soda
Cinnamon
Cloves
1 cup cognac or liqueur
Ground raisins
½ kg olive oil

Yogurt cake

Cream together the butter and sugar and then add the egg yolks and yogurt. Mix together the flour, baking powder and lemon zest and beat the egg whites separately.

Add the flour all in one, with the egg whites, to the yogurt mixture. Stir well together and pour into a buttered tin.

Bake in a moderate oven for about 1 hour.

1 ½ cups sugar
1 cup butter
2 cups flour
1 ½ cups yogurt
5 eggs
2 tsp baking powder
2 tsp lemon zest

Orange cake

Puree two whole oranges in your blender. Add the sugar, eggs, milk, semolina, baking powder and chopped almonds.

Bake the mixture in a moderate oven for 1 ¼ hours. Meanwhile prepare the syrup and pour it over the cake when you take it out of the oven.

2 oranges
1 cup milk
3 eggs
3 tbs semolina
1 cup sugar
320 gr almonds
1 tsp baking powder

Syrup:
1 cup sugar
1 cup water
Orange peel

Risogalo
(milk rice pudding)

Put the milk, rice, a little salt and half of the sugar into a saucepan and boil over a low heat until the rice has softened. Meanwhile, beat the egg yolks with the remaining sugar until the mixture is white. When the rice mixture has thickened, remove it from the heat and slowly add the egg mixture, beating continuously. Replace it on the very low heat and beat the mixture until it becomes homogeneous in texture, taking care not to let it boil. Remove from the heat and either serve hot in little bowls, or dust with cinnamon and leave to go cold.

1½ litres milk
1 cup rice
3 egg yolks
6 tbs sugar
Ground cinnamon
Salt

Easter koulourakia

Sieve the flour and mix in the vanilla. Beat the butter with the sugar and add the eggs one by one. Dissolve the ammonia in the milk and add to the mixture along with the flour, all in one. When the mixture is consolidated, knead it with your hands to form an elastic, non-sticky dough. Form sausages about half the thickness of a finger and form them into various shapes, such as snails, plaits, wheels etc. Put them on an oiled baking sheet and brush with beaten egg yolk. Bake in a moderate oven for about 20-25 minutes, until golden brown.

6 eggs
1/2 kg sugar
1 1/2 kg flour
50 gr ammonia
320 gr butter
1 envelope vanilla

Tsoureki made with yeast

Beat the sugar and egg yolks well together, and beat the whites separately. Put the flour into a bowl, make a well in the centre and add the yeast dissolved in a little warm water. Then, slowly add the beaten yolks and sugar, the stiff egg whites and finally the warmed, thinned cream.

Mix well to a dough and leave in a warm place until it has risen. Knead well again and if it sticks to your hands rub them with a little melted butter.

Form the tsourekia into shapes (half-moons, snails, bars) and leave them to rise again. When they are ready, brush them with beaten egg and scatter over the almond slivers. Bake in the oven at 200 C for about half an hour.

1 kg flour
350 gr sugar
1/2 kg cream
6 eggs
1/2 tsp ground machlepi
80 gr yeast
1/2 cup water
A few slivers of almonds

Tsoureki made with sourdough

The evening before you intend to make the tsourekia, mix the sourdough with ½ kg of flour. Leave overnight in a bowl to rise. Next morning, **divide the ingredients into two** – i.e. 5 eggs, ½ kg sugar, 250 gr cream, 750 gr milk. Beat the egg yolks with half the sugar and the egg whites with the other half. Mix together with the risen sourdough and add as much flour as needed to form a light mixture like that of a cake. Place in a warm spot to rise until it has almost doubled in bulk. Now add the other half of the ingredients to the risen dough, knead and form into tsourekia, in any shape you prefer (plaits, half-moons, snails etc). Place them on a clean cloth and leave in a warm place to rise. When they are ready, put them on an oiled baking dish, brush the surfaces with beaten egg and bake until they are golden brown.

3 kg flour
10 eggs
1 kg sugar
500 gr cream
1½ cups milk
About 1 cup sourdough

Orange koulourakia

Mix the baking powder with the flour and dissolve the baking soda in one small cup of orange juice. Beat the oil together with the sugar in your mixer and when the sugar has dissolved, add 2 eggs. Add the orange juice and dissolved baking soda and, gradually, the flour. When the mixture is thick, remove it from the mixer and knead it with your hands, incorporating the remaining flour. Form little koulouria in whatever shapes you prefer, and place them on an oiled baking sheet. To give them a gloss, brush with beaten egg before putting them in the oven. Bake at a moderate temperature until they are golden brown.

1 cup orange juice

1 cup oil

3 eggs

200 gr sugar

2 tsp baking powder

½ tsp baking soda

1 kg flour

Ladokouloura

Beat the olive oil and the orange juice together and add the sugar, ammonia dissolved in the raki, and one cup of water in which you have boiled the cinnamon.

Slowly add the flour and knead to a soft and pliable dough. Form into long sausages with your hands, roll them in the sesame and then cut off pieces 10-12 cms in length; form them into the shape of an S.

Place them on an oiled baking dish so that they do not stick, and bake in the oven for about 1 hour, until golden brown.

4 cups fine flour
1 cup orange juice
3 cups sugar
1 tbs ammonia
1 cup raki
1 little stick of cinnamon
2 cups sesame
2 cups olive oil

Melomakarona

6 cups flour

2 cups olive oil

1 cup icing sugar

1 cup milk

1 cup orange juice

1 tsp orange zest

1 tsp cinnamon

1 tsp ground clove

½ cup chopped walnuts

1 tsp baking soda

1 tsp baking powder

Syrup:

2 cups water

1 cup honey

1 cup sugar

Beat the oil well together with the icing sugar. Add the zest and the orange juice into which you have mixed the baking soda, cinnamon, clove, walnuts and milk. Then slowly add the flour mixed with the baking powder to form a soft dough. Now form the melomakarona into circular or elliptical shapes and place them on an oiled baking sheet. Bake in a moderate oven for about 30 minutes.

Meanwhile, make the syrup as follows: Boil the water in a saucepan and add the sugar and honey. When the syrup is ready, and still warm, dunk the melomakarona into it and remove immediately with a slotted spoon.

Arrange them on a plate and scatter over them a mixture of the chopped walnuts, sesame and cinnamon.

Kouloura made with grape must

Beat the oil with the sugar well together in your mixer and gradually add the grape must, lye, cognac, cinnamon and clove. Then slowly add the flour and before the dough is formed, add the lemon juice in which you have dissolved the baking soda. Add the remaining flour, but do not allow the mixture to become too stiff. Now form kouloura and place them on an oiled baking tin. Bake at first at 200 C, and then reduce the temperature to 180 and bake until they are a nice golden brown.

1 ½ cups grape must

1 cup oil

1 cup sugar

1 wine glass of lye

½ wine glass of lemon juice

1 tsp baking soda

1 tsp ground cinnamon

1 tsp ground clove

1½ kg flour

Grape must jelly

Sieve the ash, add it to the must and boil together. Leave it to cool and settle for several hours or overnight.

Next day, strain it well and pass it through a very fine sieve. Then take a little of the must and mix it with the flour so as to form a batter. Return the must to the heat and let it boil for 15 minutes. Then add the batter very slowly, beating continuously.

Boil the mixture until it is well thickened. Pour the mixture while hot into bowls or plates, and sprinkle with chopped walnuts, cinnamon and sesame. Leave to cool, and serve as it is or cut into portions.

5 kg grape must
4 cups flour
½ kg potash
Walnuts
Cinnamon

Isli

Prepare the filling by mixing all the ingredients together. Then mix the oil with the sugar and slowly add the flour which you have previously mixed with the salt and baking powder. Form a dough by adding water until a soft mass is achieved. Take pieces of the mixture about the size of a walnut, make a hole in the centre of each with your finger and put in 1 tsp of the filling. Close the dough well around the filling and place them on an oiled baking sheet with the join downwards. Bake at 200 C for about 50 minutes, until they are browned. Meanwhile, prepare the syrup by mixing all the ingredients together and letting them boil for about 5 minutes. Let the syrup cool and then pour it over the 'isli' when you take them out of the oven.

2 cups oil

1 cup of water

2 tbs sugar

Pinch of salt

1 little envelope of baking powder

1 kg flour

Filling:

1 ½ cups chopped walnuts

2-3 cloves, ground

2 tsp cinnamon

2 tbs sugar

Syrup:

1 cup sugar

1 cup honey

1 ½ cups of water

½ cup cognac

Samousades

Pastry:

1 kg flour

5 tbs oil

2 small glasses of raki

1 cup orange juice

1 pinch of salt

About 1 ½ cups of warm water

Filling:

800 gr almonds or walnuts, chopped

½ cup sesame

4 tbs sugar

1 tsp ground cinnamon

½ tsp ground clove

Syrup:

2 cups of water

1 cup sugar

1 cup honey

1 cinnamon stick

Prepare the pastry: mix together the flour and salt in a bowl, and make a well in the centre. Add the orange juice, oil, raki and water and mix to a moderate to firm dough. Let it rest for a while and in the meantime, prepare the filling by mixing all the ingredients together. Divide the dough into 4 balls and roll them out into thin sheets. Brush the sheets with oil and spread a quarter of the filling on each. Now roll them up into a long sausage and then cut it into sections like small baklava. Place them on an oiled baking sheet, brush with oil and bake them in a moderate oven for about half an hour. While they are cooking, make the syrup by boiling all the ingredients together until they thicken slightly. Coat the samousades with syrup when they are removed from the oven and if liked, dust with cinnamon and sesame.

'Vrahakia' ('little rocks')

Melt the chocolate in a bain-marie and add the almonds. Take spoonfuls of the mixture and drop them onto greaseproof paper. Leave for several hours to set. When they are ready, they can be wrapped in cellophane or aluminium foil.

1 kg chocolate for cake covering

800 gr whole shelled almonds

Kourambiedes

Beat the oil and sugar well together in a bowl. Add the baking soda, lemon, walnuts, and finally the flour in stages, to make a fairly firm dough. Form into shapes, either round or whatever you prefer, and place them on a lightly oiled baking tin.

Bake in a preheated oven for about 40 minutes. When they are ready, remove from the heat and sprinkle over a little flower water, then dust them thickly with powdered sugar (use a sieve).

1 kg flour

2 tbs sugar

3 tbs chopped walnuts

1/2 tsp baking soda

1/2 lemon (juice and zest required)

1/2 kg powdered sugar

Flower water

2 cups oil

Semolina halva

Heat the oil in a pan and add the semolina. Mix well until the semolina begins to roast and take on a dark brown colour. In another pan, boil the water with the sugar, stirring it for about 5 minutes until the sugar has dissolved and then add the lemon zest. When the syrup is ready add it slowly to the pan containing the halva, and let it boil for a little while until the semolina has absorbed it. At the same time, add the almonds. Cover the halva with a clean tea towel and let it cool. Serve dusted with the cinnamon.

1 cup semolina

1/2 cup oil

100 gr blanched almonds

cinnamon

Syrup:

1 1/2 cups sugar

2 1/2 cups of water

Zest of a lemon

Fresh walnut spoon sweet

1 1/2 kg fresh walnuts

1 1/2 kg blanched almonds

1 1/2 kg sugar

3 cups of water

1 glass of lemon juice

Skin the walnuts, wash them and boil them until they are soft. Then put them in a pan with fresh water and change it every eight hours over the space of two days. When the walnuts have lost their bitterness, boil the sugar with the water for 10 minutes and add the walnuts and the almonds to boil in the syrup for about 7 minutes. Turn off the heat and leave the walnuts to stand in their syrup for a day. Then, replace the pan on the heat and boil until the syrup has thickened well. Finally, add the lemon juice, let the mixture boil for 5 minutes and the spoon sweet is ready.

Sour cherry spoon sweet

Wash the cherries and remove the stones, using a special instrument if you have one. Spread them out in a pan in alternate layers with the sugar. Leave for about 2-3 hours and then add the water and boil until the mixture thickens.

When it is ready, add the lemon; after cooling, pour into glass jars and store in a cool place.

1 kg sour cherries
1 ½ kg sugar
1 cup of water
1 tsp lemon

Sour cherry drink

Cut off the stalks of the cherries, wash them and remove the stones. Puree them in a blender. Place the puree in a fine sieve and press out all the juice; boil it with the lemon juice and the sugar until a thickish syrup is obtained, as in spoon sweets.

When it is ready, allow to cool and then pour into clean, dry bottles.

1 kg sour cherries
1 kg sugar
Juice of 1 lemon

Cherry
spoon sweet

1 kg cherries, 1 kg sugar, ½ cup water

Select firm cherries which will withstand
boiling. Remove the stalks, wash the cherries
and dry them with a cloth. Put the sugar and water
into a pan, turn on the heat and as soon as the sugar has
dissolved (without letting it boil) add the cherries. Now bring them
to the boil once or twice and remove from the heat. When they have
cooled, remove the fruit from the pan with a slotted spoon and put
them on a plate. Then return the syrup to the heat and boil it until
it is well thickened. Add the cherries again and bring to the boil a
couple of times. Add a little lemon juice and remove the pan from
the heat. When the spoon sweet is cold, pour it into clean jars.

Quince spoon sweet

Take large quinces, rub them on a sieve and cut them into small strips. Put them into a pan with the water and bring to the boil a couple of times, until they soften.

Add the sugar and boil over a high heat, until the syrup forms, taking care that the quinces retain their yellow colour and do not redden. Finally, add the lemon juice and after boiling for a few minutes, remove from the heat and add the almonds.

1 kg quinces
1 kg sugar
2 cups of water
1 tsp lemon juice
½ cup blanched almonds

Little pear spoon sweet

Wash the pears, peel them and cut off the stems. Remove the pips carefully, so that each fruit remains in one piece.

Put the pears in a bowl of cold water and add the juice of two lemons. Place an almond inside every pear. Now put them into a pan, add water to half cover them, and half of the sugar.

Let them boil and then add the remaining sugar and the juice of 2 lemons. Continue boiling until the syrup has formed. Turn off the heat, allow them to cool a little and fill them into jars.

2 kg small pears
2 kg sugar
4 lemons
As many almonds as pears

Orange spoon sweet

Rub the oranges on a grater and then remove their peel in vertical sections. Score the oranges vertically and remove the peel from the oranges.

Wind the peel into rolls and secure them with toothpicks. Now boil the rolls for 5 minutes, change the water, boil them again and strain them.

Put the sugar into a pan with 2 litres of water and boil it until the syrup is almost formed. Then, add the rolls of orange peel and leave them to simmer for 15 minutes until the syrup is thick.

10 oranges
1 kg sugar

Small aubergine spoon sweet

Wash the aubergines, cut off the stalks and make an incision along the length of each. Place them in water for 24 hours, changing the water every 8 hours.

When they have sweetened, drain off the water; insert two almonds into each incision and push a clove into the top of each aubergine. Boil the sugar with the water, cinnamon and a few cloves for 5 minutes. Add the aubergines and boil for another 5 minutes. Turn off the heat and leave the aubergines in the syrup for 24 hours. A fterwards, bring to the boil again over a high heat, remove the scum, add the lemon and let it boil once or twice again to thicken up the syrup.

1 kg small aubergines

1 ½ kg sugar

½ kg blanched almonds

2 sticks cinnamon

Whole cloves

1 tsp lemon juice

2 cups of water

Grape spoon sweet

Remove the stalks from the grapes, which should be selected for their freshness and firmness. Wash them, and put them into a pan in alternate layers with the sugar. Leave them for one night so that the moisture exudes from the fruit and the sugar dissolves.

Next day, boil the mixture until the sugar has completely dissolved and a syrup has formed. Finally, add the geranium leaves, let the mixture boil for a short while again and then remove it from the heat. When it is cold, pour it into clean jars to store.

1 kg sultana grapes

1 kg sugar

2-3 leaves of sweet geranium (Pelargonium odoratissimum)

Bitter orange spoon sweet

Wash the oranges, dry them and rub them on a grater to take off a little of their surfaces. Place them in cold water. Score them vertically and take off the peel in sections. Take each piece of peel separately and wind it into a roll with the white pith on the inside; thread all the rolls onto a string, using a thick needle. Tie the ends so that they cannot

1 kg bitter oranges

1 kg sugar

unthread. Boil them in a large amount of water until they soften. Now place them in cold water and leave for a whole day, changing the water 3 or 4 times so that the peel loses its bitterness. Drain well and lay the string on a cloth to drain further. Place them in a pan and cover them with 1 cup of sugar and 1 cup of water. Bring to the boil and, shortly before the syrup begins to form, remove the string. Continue boiling until the spoon sweet is ready. Allow to cool and pack into clean, dry jars.

Apricot marmalade

Choose firm, ripe apricots. Wash them well, cut them up and remove the stones. Put them in a pan with one cup of water and boil them until they have softened and become a puree.

Process them in your blender, to ensure that no pieces of skin have remained, and put the puree back into the saucepan with the sugar. Boil, stirring well with a wooden spoon so that the mixture does not stick to the bottom of the pan.

The marmalade has set if it coats the back of a spoon and stays there when held downwards. Now add the lemon juice. Let it boil once or twice again and then remove the pan from the heat. Pour the marmalade, when cold, into clean, dry jars.

1 kg apricots
1 kg sugar
1 tsp lemon juice
1 cup of water

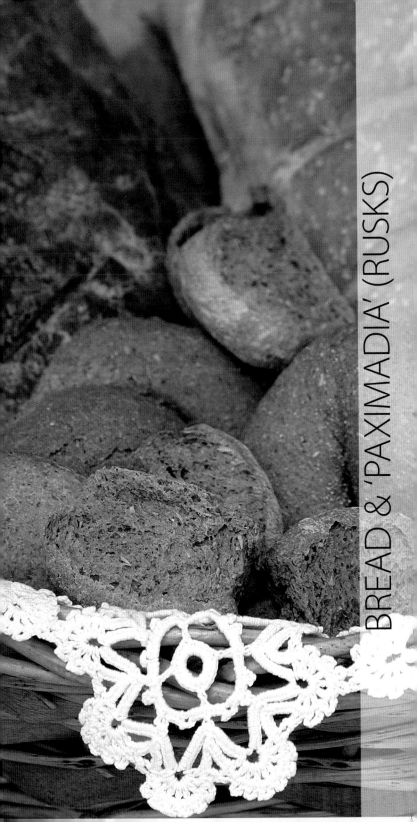

BREAD & 'PAXIMADIA' (RUSKS)

Bread made with sourdough

The evening before, 'restart' the sourdough by adding 1 kg flour and a little water to make a very soft dough (it should, however, not be runny). Put it into a bowl and cover it with ½ kg flour. Now place the bowl in a plastic bag, close it well and cover it with a warm cloth.

Next day, when the mixture is well risen, add the remaining flour, oil, salt and, very slowly, water so that the mixture takes on the appearance of 'mastiha' (gum).

After kneading the dough very well for quite a while and periodically wetting your hands, form it into loaves (round or elongated), wrap them with a clean cotton or linen tea towel and place a blanket on top. Leave to rise in a warm place. After about 3-4 hours, when the bread is well risen, place them on a (preferably) metal baking tray lined with greaseproof paper.

Bake in a preheated oven, at first at 180 C and then at 200 C, for about one hour.

If liked, sunflower seeds, pine nuts, raisins, olives etc. can be added to the bread.

2 ½ kg flour (1½ kg wholemeal and 1 kg white)

½ cup oil

3 tsp salt

1 cup sourdough

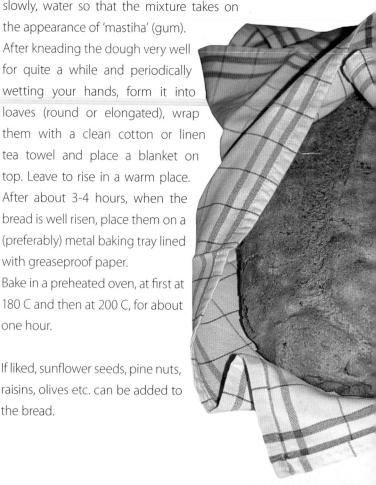

Lagana

Dissolve the yeast in a little warm water, mix it well with a little flour to form a thick cream and leave it in a warm place to bubble.

Put the flour into a bowl and make a well in the centre; add the oil, sugar, salt, yeast and a little warm water.

Mix together, adding warm water at intervals, until a dough is obtained; it should not be sticky. Form it into a ball, cover it with a cotton cloth and leave it in a warm place to rise.

When the dough is ready, cut small pieces and roll out each to an oval with a thickness of ½ cm. Place them on an oiled dish, cover again with a cloth, and leave to rise. Finally, push your fingers into the surface to form little holes, brush with oil, sprinkle over the sesame, and bake in a moderate oven until they are browned.

1 kg flour
2 tsp fresh yeast
2 tbs sugar
1 cup oil
1 tsp salt
Sesame
Warm water

Sweet rusks made with sourdough

3 kg flour

700 gr sugar

3 cups oil

300 gr sesame

½ a little bottle of cinnamon oil

2 tsp ground cloves

2 tsp mastiha

100 gr coriander

1 tsp cinnamon

1 tsp pepper

Sourdough (about 1 cup)

'Restart' the sourdough by kneading it **with ¾** kg of flour and a little water. Leave overnight to rise. The next morning, mix it to a dough with the other ingredients, apart from the sesame. Form elongated loaves and cut them them vertically into slices, so that you can separate the paximadia from one another later. Scatter the sesame over a tray or work surface and roll the loaves in it. Cover and leave in a warm place to rise. When the loaves are ready, bake them at first in a moderate oven (180 C) and then increase the temperature. As soon as they have browned, turn off the heat and leave them to cool. They can be eaten when they are soft. If liked, however, they can be dried and hardened by returning them to the oven at a low heat, until all the moisture has evaporated and they become crunchy.

Rusks with raisins

Beat the sugar and the oil and add the orange and cinnamon juices (make the latter by boiling 2-3 cinnamon sticks in water). Now add the ammonia, clove, cinnamon, raisins, almonds and the flour mixed with the baking powder. Mix well to a dough with your hands and form into long sticks. Score them deeply and vertically with a knife to form slices and bake in a moderate oven until they brown. When you take them from the oven, separate off the slices and then put them on a baking dish. Return to the oven at a low temperature, until all the moisture has evaporated and they become crunchy.

1 cup oil

1 cup sugar

1 cup raisins

1 cup almonds

1 cup orange juice

1 cup cinnamon juice

½ cup flour

1 tsp cinnamon

1 tsp clove

1 envelope ammonia

1 envelope baking powder

Little rusks

Mix the sugar and oil well together. Add the baking soda dissolved in some of the orange juice, then the rest of the juice and the vanilla. Now, gradually add the flour, having first mixed it with the baking powder. When a stiff dough has formed, shape pieces into paximadakia (little rusks) and bake them in a medium oven until they have browned.

1 cup oil

1 cup orange juice

1 cup sugar

1 envelope baking powder

Baking soda

1 envelope vanilla

As much flour as needed